For Candy

The author of this text
subscribes to no particular religion or
spiritual dogma. The author only wishes
to pursue the still beating voice of truth
within his own heart.

This book is the interpretation
of spiritual, esoteric and occult
concepts as understood by the author
to make sense of these ideas
within the context of his own life.

The only confirmation that can be secured
of any of the material therein must be and can
only be done by the reader and the reader alone.

PI &
THE ENGLISH ALPHABET
Vol. 2

A B C D E F G H I J K L M
N O P Q R S T U V W X Y Z
1 2 3 4 5 6 7 6 5 4 3 2 1

by Marty Leeds

"In all chaos there is a cosmos, in all disorder a secret order."
~ Carl Jung

CONTENTS

I - Appreciation
II - A Universal Picture
III - Helpful Resources
IV - VI - References & Sources

"If we don't know life, how can we know death?"
~ Confucius

"A human being is a part of a whole, called by us *universe*, a part limited in time and space. He experiences himself, his thoughts and feelings as something separated from the rest ... a kind of optical delusion of his consciousness. This delusion is a kind of prison for us, restricting us to our personal desires and to affection for a few persons nearest to us. Our task must be to free ourselves from this prison by widening our circle of compassion to embrace all living creatures and the whole of nature in its beauty."
~ Albert Einstein

"The fountain-head of strength from which one may draw is inexhaustible."
~ Rudolf Steiner

"I don't need faith. I have experience."
~ Joseph Cambell

"The word *know* comes to us from the word *gnosis* meaning divine wisdom, or mystical insight. Using the English cipher, AWAKE (14135), DANCE (41135) and KNOW (3124) are all numerical anagrams for Pi (3.1415 or 3.142). To truly live is to *dance*, to *know* and to be *awake*. You ask, Art thou serious with all of this number magic? and my response is Yes! For thou is art."
~ Claudia Pavonis

If you think you're too small to make a difference, you haven't spent time with a mosquito.
~ African proverb

"Are you a traveling man?"

INTRODUCTION

Gematria is the ancient art of assigning numbers to letters to reveal deeper meaning and significance to words. Many prominent languages that existed throughout history (Sanskrit - the oldest known language, Hebrew, and Greek) assigned numbers to the letters, or characters, of their alphabets. Symbols, glyphs, characters, and/or letters were not simply arbitrary constructions of lines and circles. These letters, their sounds and their geometry *spoke* of the hidden cosmological principles composing the universe. To those who mastered the art of gematria (derived from the word "geometry"), language was understood as the medium that withheld the truth and proof of a hidden, intelligent force, often deemed "God." God, in many cultures, began the construction of the universe with a voice, a sound or vibratory essence. We can find myriad examples of this within hundreds of cultures (Hindu and Hebrew / Christian genesis stories being two prime examples). The Greek's celebrated the *Logos* which, when translated into English, finds us a bevy of varying definitions; geometry, ratio, symbol, reason and word. This *logos* is the animating principle or force existing throughout the universe. In the Holy Bible, John 1:1, this is known as the *Word* of God. In order to understand this holy *Word* of God, if our definitions serve us justly, then we must understand *geometry, ratios, symbols* and *reason,* which, when combined, create the foundation of the very *words* we speak.

The Confusion of Tongues is the initial fragmentation of human languages described in the Book of Genesis, as a result of the construction of the Tower of Babel (and where we derive the term to *babble,* or speak incoherently). This singular, often called the Adamic language, was supposedly the language spoken in the paradise of the Garden of Eden. In *The Divine Comedy,* Dante claims that Adam addressed God as "I" rather than "El." This poetic interpretation of our primordial language is extremely important. In order to fully understand the great *Word* of God, he must first understand the true nature of whom is doing the speaking and to whom he is speaking to.

In undergoing the study of the philosophy of mathematics, one will eventually come to the paradox of zero and one. Everything must have come from one thing, and yet, how did that one thing spring from no-thing? How did the one thing then become many things? This philosophy will inevitably, *if the pursuit is consistent,* lead one to the oneness and wholeness of the circle. The circle presents us with the intuitive understanding that, out of the infinitely many, there is but *one.*

1

The story of creation casts its shadow upon every event in the universe. This is the story of the one becoming many and the many being one. This philosophy can be understood simply by the phrase *E Pluribus Unum* or "Out of many, one." Conversely, we can see this statement also means "Out of one, many." The allegory of the Confusion of Tongues leads us to the understanding that though they're are over 6,000 languages spoken today and though we all speak with different inflections and dialects, the voice we bring to this world is but one voice. It is the voice of the Logos, telling its same story in myriad ways.

The Freemasonic legend of Hiram Abiff, a story not told in the Bible, is the lamentation of the loss of the holy Masonic *Word* with the death of Hiram, a Master Mason and builder of Solomon's Temple. Many Masons throughout history have tried to recover this Lost Word to no avail. Could the Lost Masonic Word not be a singular *Word* at all and instead be an allegory about Hiram understanding the *Logos* or archetypal nature of language itself? Did Hiram come to know this *Word* of God through number, symbol, reason and ratio?

Albert Einstein once exclaimed, "Creativity is intelligence having fun." If there is an intelligent force, a Grand Architect, who underlies the entire universe, then we might assume that when composing the world, this creator was being *creative* with *creation*. Heraclitus exclaimed "The Aeon is at play with colored balls" or *The universe is at play with sound, symbol, number and geometry*. Maybe to understand the great Logos of God, we need to learn to do as he did; *be creative* with symbol, number and language. The divine work of God is in plain sight, though the full grasp of his works are hidden. In order to understand the workings of the universe, one must travel into the dark inner landscapes of the self. One must go into the depths of the hidden to find the proof and divine truths of God's work. The word *occult* has acquired much baggage over the years. *Occult* simply means "hidden" and, like the word *culture*, has its roots in the word *cult*. Alchemy was known as the "black arts" and is often synonymous with *black magic*. Finding the *hidden*, or *occult*, God is to be found by traversing one's inner landscape searching for the *magica*l light within the *black*ness of the interiorized self. If understood that the search for God must be done by traveling into one's own dark recesses, then the negative connotations of the word *occult* simply fall away. God is hidden within us all and only if one is willing to brave the darkness, will he comprehend the true light. "He who wants pearls has to dive in the sea."
- Kurdish proverb

2

THE WHOLE PI

"If why is the question, Pi is the answer." - Claudia Pavonis

"To come to an UNDERSTANDING of this world, you must first know what you are STANDING UNDER and of course what is UNDER what you are STANDING on - and these are the Heavens and the Earth. By contemplating these two eternal concepts you may just come to the UNDERSTANDING that they balance each other by nothing more and nothing less than yourself."
- Claudia Pavonis

Pi has long been defined as the ratio of a circle's circumference to its diameter.

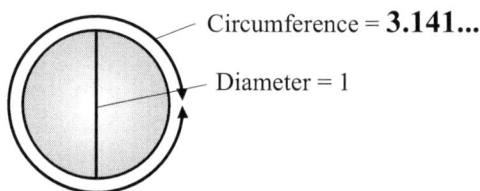

Circumference = **3.141...**

Diameter = 1

A mathematical constant represented by the Greek letters:

$$\pi \Pi$$

Pi is an infinite, *transcendental,* and irrational number. Pi unfolds its decimals in a seemingly random fashion, though we know they are anything but random since the ratio of a circle's circumference to its diameter will always be consistent. Why is this number so elusive?

How can irrationality be consistently rational? Pi leads us to a grand paradox of thought and asks us to *transcend* our states of mind and frames of *understanding.* Pi is a transcendental number and transcendental means to "climb over or surmount." Pi is a Holy Mountain, a mathematical constant waiting for us to brave its heights. To try to tackle Pi in a merely quantitative way will lead to dead ends and countless headaches. The irrational and rational paradoxical nature of Pi is asking us a question: What do we wish to see? Do we choose to see the world as ir*ratio*nal and chaotic or *ratio*nal and beautiful? Notice the common thing between these two extremes is a *ratio.* Pi is no problem at all, in fact, it could quite possibly be the answer to our questions. It might just be the most *rational* thing in our world. The Freemasonic expression *ordo ab chao* is a philosophy certainly fitting when dealing with Pi.

THE SOUND OF MUSIC

Music is a universal language. More so than any other art, music is the one form of communication that breaks all barriers. One does not need to know how to play an instrument, how to write musical notation, nor understand what language a particular song is sung in to appreciate a musical performance. The frequencies and vibrations of sound enter the canals of our ingeniously crafted ear drums, eliciting emotions, memories and feelings that sometimes even move us into an ecstatic frenzy of dance. Understanding the phenomenon of language and how it is we communicate though sound, has been the cause of frustration for linguists and philologists over the years. It is truly a miracle how we can string a series of sounds together and have these sounds then received and correlated to another person's internal dictionary. Communication through speech is something that we participate in every day and yet we hardly ever stop to even consider how it works.

Sound has no agenda. It is neither bad nor good. Sound is merely a wavelength vibrating at a particular frequency, and what we do with these wavelengths is up to us. *We choose* whether to make them harmonious or dissonant. Our speech allows us the freedom to either wow a loved one with beautiful poetry or corrupt entire nations with propagandist oratory. Language and words are powerful tools, even mightier than the sword as we've been told.

Languages are like flowers. Each one is different and beautiful in its own way. Each one has its own pedals, stems and colors but no matter how different these flowers are, every single one grows from a fundamental mathematical sequence. Without the foundation of mathematics, the language of God according to Galileo, flowers would not know how to grow to receive the optimal light and rain. If the mineral, vegetable and animal worlds operate under the strict laws of mathematics, then we should assume that the constructions of languages, however they are formed, should follow a fundamental mathematical pattern as well. The thousands of languages that are spoken across the world today are but branches of a single tree, uniting at the trunk, born from a single seed. No matter how different we may sound, our voice is but one voice. Every single language speaks the voice of our universal creator and this creator has chosen human beings to sound its glory, a responsibility we must not take lightly.

THE KEY

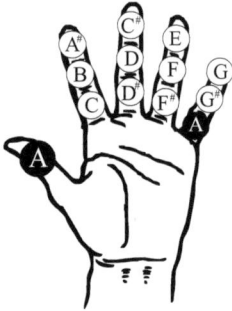

B FLAT
2 6 2 1 7 = 18

A SHARP
1 6 6 1 5 3 = 22

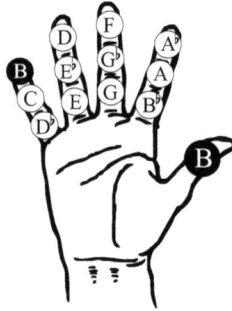

ALPHA
א ALEF
"Master"

of the

BET
ב BET
"House"

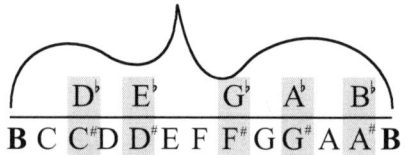

A	B	C	D	E	F	G	H	I	J	K	L	M	N	O	P	Q	R	S	T	U	V	W	X	Y	Z
1	2	3	4	5	6	7	6	5	4	3	2	1	1	2	3	4	5	6	7	6	5	4	3	2	1

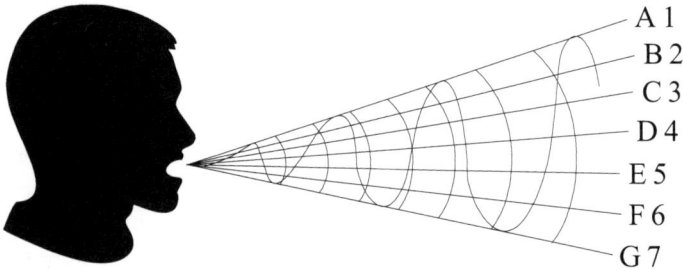

A 1
B 2
C 3
D 4
E 5
F 6
G 7

KEY
3 5 2 = **3.5 X 2 = SEVEN**

SEVEN
6 5 5 5 1 = **22**

22 / SEVEN = π 3.142...

"All the world's a stage, and all the men and women merely players: they
have their exits and their entrances; and one man in his time plays many
parts, his acts being *seven* ages."
~ William Shakespeare

5

THE CIPHER

We will be using the cipher shown below throughout the text so taking the time to internalize this cryptogram is most advised.

A B C D E F G H I J K L M
N O P Q R S T U V W X Y Z
1 2 3 4 5 6 7 6 5 4 3 2 1

In Volume 1 of this text, we de-constructed the English Alphabet, placing the letters on our hands, splitting our alphabet at the M and N, giving us 13 letters per side. We walked up to the number 7 on each side of our alphabet, resting on the letters G and T, and then we walked back down to 1 to find the corresponding numbers for the letters of our alphabet as shown above. Through separating the primes and non-primes, we also constructed Pi on both sides, or hands, of our alphabet that combined to give us the Tetragrammaton, or what was known by the alchemists and Kabbalists as the Holy Name of God.

In this volume, we are going to look at the cipher in an entirely new way. Language is nothing more than sound, and sound is nothing more than vibration. Vibrations tend to completion in 7 stages, and since the words we speak are vibrations, we should assume that speech and the construction of our alphabet should no doubt follow this *Law of Seven*. Adding 1 through 7 yields us the number **28**. (1+2+3+4+5+6+7 = **28**) In the first volume we multiplied these 7 numbers to "square the circle" of the Earth and Moon to find the combined radius of 5,040 miles. In this text we will use this **28** as a guide to correlate the chromatic music scale with the letters of our alphabet to the sections of our two hands. For as we know, we have **28** sections, or phalanges of our two hands.

The chromatic scale (*Chroma* means "color" or the 7 primary colors) is composed of 12 notes with the 13th note being the octave. The first seven letters of the alphabet (A - G) find us the 7 notes of the major scale. Since we have already split our alphabet into 13 letters a side, let's put the chromatic scale, root to octave, making a total of 13 notes, atop our alphabet. Since we are dealing with the "**A**"lpha "**B**"et, let's put "**A**" on our left hand and "**B**" on our right (The root of **A** being our left thumb and the root of **B** being our right - illustration on the following page).

6

A A#B C C#D D#E F F#G G#A B CDbD EbE FGb GAb A BbB
A B C D E F G H I J K L M N O P Q R S T U V W X Y Z

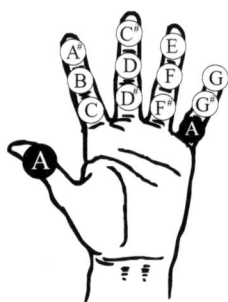

B FLAT
2 6 2 1 7 = **18**

A SHARP
1 6 6 1 5 3= **22**

ALPHA   of the   BET
א ALEF   ב BET
"Master"   "House"

Now we have the root to octave chromatic scales of **A** on our left hand and **B** on our right. The first two letters of the Hebrew alphabet are <u>Alef</u> and <u>Bet</u> or <u>Beth</u>. <u>Alef</u> means "master" or "ox" and <u>Bet</u> means "house." We can put the two meanings of our Alefbet together and find the phrase "Master of the House." Our two hands represent the commanding will of the God within us. What we choose to do with these hands is literally *in our own hands,* for we are indeed the *Master of the House.* Putting the "**A**"lpha on our left hand and the "**B**"et on our right leaves us one note between our hands. This note has two distinctions, B Flat and A Sharp. Using our cipher, these two distinctions yield two very interesting numbers which leads to an even more interesting numerical correlation:

B FLAT   A SHARP   ROSE   CROSS
2 6 2 1 7=**18**   1 6 6 1 5 3 = **22**   5 2 6 5 =**18**   3 5 2 6 6 = **22**

The Rose Cross is a symbol largely associated with the semi-mythical Christian Rosenkreuz, alchemist and founder of the Rosicrucian Order. The symbol of the Rose Cross was adorned by members of the Hermetic Order of the Golden Dawn, and several Rose Cross' followers were linked to many of the secret societies throughout history. Alchemy and Freemasonry wielded the tools of a compass and square to understand their inner god. Understanding measurement was quintessential, for God was indeed a *Grand Architect. Rose* sums to 18 and *Cross* sums to 22. 18 x 22 = **396**. **396** multiplied by our ten fingers yields us **3,960**. The radius of the Earth is **3,960** miles. Some occultists even believe that the Earth's vibration hums the tone of B flat.

7

```
1 2 3 4 5 6 7 8  9 10 11 12 1
A A#B C C#D D#E  F F#G G#A
A B C D E F G H  I  J  K  L  M
1 2 3 4 5 6 7              1
```

Above we have the 13 notes, root to octave, of the A major scale placed over the first 13 letters of our alphabet. Since A is 1, we can name the octave of A, or the 13th note, 1 as well to maintain consistency. As we walked up the 7 notes of the major scale we rested on the G. The next major note should be the octave A, but since we spread out the chromatic scale on the top row, to accommodate for our sharps and flats, this now puts A atop our 13th letter M. When we walk from G back down to the A/M being One/1, we can assign numbers to the rest of our letters: H, I, J, K and L, being 6, 5, 4, 3 and 2 back to *One*:

```
  1 2 3 4 5 6 7 8  9 10 11 12 1
 (A)A#B C C#D D#E  F F#G G(A)
 (A)B C D E F G H  I  J  K L(M)
  1 2 3 4 5 6 7  6 5 4 3 2 1
```
"I am One"

The A and M both equaling *One* in this cipher, if viewed creatively, recalls another interesting deific phrase "I AM ONE."

Since our left hand is nothing more than a mirror of our right hand, we can mirror the Alpha of our left hand over to the Beta of our right hand, creating the perfect mirror symmetry needed to find the numbers for the second half of our alphabet.

```
A A#B C C#D D#E  F F#G G#A   B C D♭D E♭E F G♭ G A♭ A B♭B
A B C D E F G H  I  J  K L M  N O P Q R S T U V W X Y Z
1 2 3 4 5 6 7 6 5 4 3 2 1  1 2 3 4 5 6 7 6 5 4 3 2 1
```

Using the **28** sections of our fingers as our guide has allowed us to find magic within music, symbol, math and most importantly, our alphabet. This number **28,** that is right in front of our faces, *on our two hands,* gives us a whole new way to unearth the real meaning of the *Holy Bible,* for *it is you* who is the written *Word* of God.

HOLY BIBLE
6 2 2 2 25 2 2 5 = **28**

8

THE ALPHABET

The English Alphabet as we have seen comes directly from the Hebrew alphabet, or the alef bet. Our alphabet is a foundation - 26 simple constructions of lines and arcs - that allows us to formulate our thoughts into the form of audible words. Most often we think of language as just the interweaving of these words that we use to convey our meanings, but language is much more than that. Symbols, movements and even mathematics are languages as well. Any sort of act that transmits a meaning or intention could be considered a language. Take for instance sign language. By the simple movements of hand gestures, two or more people can have lengthy discussions without a single utterance being emitted. Music notation is a language. If one is able to read musical notation, the notes of a page could be heard in one's mind without the sounds even being played, and henceforth the author of the particular piece of music can communicate to the listener reading the page. Body language is also a language. One can easily detect confidence, dis-ease, fear, or elation simply by how one presents himself bodily. Language is assuredly not just done through the letters on a page such as this one. With how much we've seen thus far relating to Pi, the symbol shown again below, you should understand that it is communicating much more to you than you may ever have thought before. This symbol represents much more than the simple mathematical ratio of a circle's circumference to its diameter. It is much more than an endless string of numbers.

$$\pi \Pi$$

Pi is, in fact, speaking to you.

The language of the Grand Architect is a language which encases all forms of communication. Every motion, every sound, every word, every thought, and every action speaks of the holiness of the world around you. Even the alphabet itself is telling you about the sacredness and divinity of the world in which you live. The alphabet wants to tell you about the *whole* thing and how truly *holy* it is.

ALPHA   BET
1 2 3 6 1 = **13**   2 5 7 = **14** | **13** | **31** | & | **14** | **41** | = 3.141 π

The alphabet seems to be really concerned with Pi. Since we use it to speak to each other, maybe we should listen *to what it has to say*.

THE EMBLEM OF ISRAEL

The state of Israel was formed in November of 1947 following the adoption of a resolution by the United Nations General Assembly. Bordering Lebanon, Syria, Egypt and Jordan, the establishment of this Jewish state has caused much pain and conflict in the region. Though Israel has signed peace treaties with Egypt and Jordan, the efforts to resolve the Israeli–Palestinian conflict have so far not resulted in peace. Our focus on this volatile area will not be political but rather numerical and symbolic. Israel can be broken up into three different Egyptian gods: *Isis*, *Ra* and *El*. These three gods are actually reflective of the Holy Trinity: Isis being the Mother, Ra being the Son and El being the Father. These three gods, abbreviated in the composite name of Israel, sum to 24, the numerical equivalent of *Earth* and *Egypt*. If we calculate the numerical equivalents for the three gods that make up the name we find they sum to **35**, not coincidentally the same numbers as Pi (**3** & **5**), as well as the numerical equivalent of Jerusalem, the nation's capital and most populous city.

ISRAEL	ISIS RA EL	JERUSALEM	PI
5 6 5 1 5 2 = **24**	5656 5 1 5 2 = **35** = 4 5 5 6 6 1 2 5 1		**35**

The emblem for Israel actually gives us the symbols needed to find the cipher for the English Alphabet.

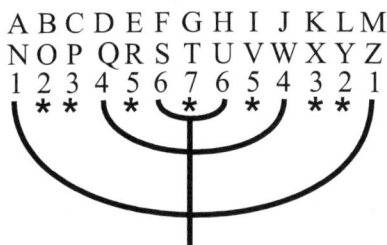

```
A B C D E F G H I J K L M
N O P Q R S T U V W X Y Z
1 2 3 4 5 6 7 6 5 4 3 2 1
  * *   *   *   *   * *
```

Notice the wreath is separated into 13 leaves and 13 leaves reflective of our split of the English Alphabet with the 7th, or central leaf, pointing up on each side representing the "Sabbaths" or our G and T. There are 24 berries, 12 on each branch summing to 24, or *Israel*. The Menorah atop the pedestal is a direct reference to the highlighted non-primes we used to find Pi in the English cipher. The letters below the pedestal are Lamed, Aleph, Resh, Shin and Yod, which spell out *Israel* in Hebrew. The Emblem of Israel is symbolic Rosetta Stone, linking Egyptian, Hebrew and English languages - but only if you know how to speak *its language*.

10

FREEDOM AND LIBERTY

Every man yearns to be free. Man wishes to pursue his own happiness, unencumbered by any restrictions made by his fellow man, his government, or any other organization or authority. The Constitution and the Bill of Rights were documents drawn up a mere few hundred years ago by the founding fathers of the United States to ensure that the people would maintain basic rights, such as religious freedom, the freedom to assemble and protest, and the right to bear arms. Throughout history, certain powers have consistently tried to usurp these ideas. Kings and dictators, presidents and influential interests have tried to steal our liberty, enslave our minds, terrorize our souls and destroy our sovereignty. The founding fathers of the United States believed in God, quite possibly because their understanding of God gave them the knowledge that freedom is inherent and implicit in every human being, a freedom to live as one wants, only restricted by the laws of nature and the acts of God.

The Thrice Great Hermes Trismegistus, author of the Hermetic Corpus and often considered to be a syncretic combination of the Egyptian god Thoth and the Greek Hermes, achieved a state of godhood by his knowledge of measurement, writing, mathematics and astrology. *Man becoming God* through altruism, passion and knowledge is known by the term *apotheosis*. Apotheosis is the state of grace reached by so many of the mystics and magis of the past. Like Hermes, George Washington himself was said to be elevated to this most austere status. Both *Hermes* and *Thoth* in our cipher sum to **28**. Holy Bible as we know sums to **28** as well. In order to maintain our freedom, we must enlighten ourselves. We must not allow the powers that be enslave our consciousness, control our destinies and indoctrinate our minds, bodies and souls. The only way to maintain freedom and liberty is to put the power in your own hands for *freedom* and *liberty* literally rests *in your hands*. The Liberty Bell rings *only when you choose to ring it.*

FREEDOM
6 5 5 5 4 2 1 = **28**

The **28** phalanges of your two hands

LIBERTY
2 5 2 5 5 7 2 = **28**

11

WE THE PEOPLE ...

The first three words of the preamble to the Constitution of the United States of America reads "We the People." This phrase was used as a means to capture the heart and spirit of a newborn nation - a nation that was no longer under the spell of a totalitarian Empire, a nation yearning to live freely, under the natural laws of God and with its government ensuring the basic rights of freedom and liberty.

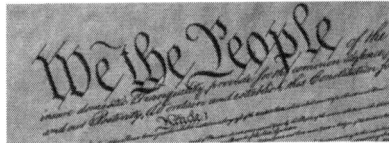

The Freemasonic founders of the United States wanted to ensure that through this opening phrase, and through the simple principles detailed in the Constitution, man would have a chance to pursue his happiness. Man would have the opportunity to find his *Heaven* right here on God's green *Earth*. The numerical equivalent of "We the People" confirms our founding fathers ambitions.

WE THE PEOPLE...	HEAVEN EARTH
4 5 7 6 5 3 5 2 3 2 5 = **47**	6 5 1 5 5 1 + 5 1 5 7 6 = **47**

Thomas Jefferson, one of America's founding fathers, prophetically reminded us "Every generation needs a revolution." Jefferson never intended this to be a statement suggesting people riot or turn to violence but instead a statement speaking of the revolution of the mind. The knowledge of our ancestors must be resurrected each generation so every generation may thrive instead of suffer under the grips of ignorance. The f oundation laid forth by our forefathers allows us to pick ourselves up by our own boot-straps and gives us the platform to rediscover our inherent freedoms by understanding the divinity of every man. *We the People* have the *Heaven* within us right here on *Earth*. Man must be free. It is the one right that is granted by God himself. No man shall lord over another for each man is a *lord*, the *lord of his own manner*, and indeed an aspect of the divine essence. The flag of the United States is stained with the blood of our past - untold wars, the genocide of native peoples and the enslavement of African-Americans are but a few of our past sins. We can not undo our past but we can relearn the knowledge of the sacred and recognize the divine nature of ourselves. *We the people* wield much power, but only if we are willing to accept and use it.

LORD & GOD

The King James Holy Bible addresses God with two names: "God" and "Lord." These two distinctions of the great name of God are pointing to two different aspects of the same phenomenon of God's greatness - the singularity and the wholeness of his work. We understood that this concept is embedded in the Greek Monad, with the point representing the singularity and the circle representing the wholeness.

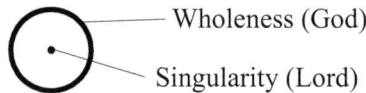

Wholeness (God)

Singularity (Lord)

Using our cipher, both God and Lord equal 13, which directly refers to the equality that you, the Lord *on Earth*, or the *singularity*, have with God or the *wholeness* in *Heaven*.

LORD   GOD
2 2 5 4 = **13** = 7 2 4

Both Lord and God come together to equal 26, which is the numerical equivalent of the Hebraic Tetragrammaton, as well as the number of letters in the English Alphabet. Lord consists of 4 letters, and God consists of 3 letters. This 3 and 4 we have previously recognized in sacred geometry with the circle representing Heaven and the number 3 and the square representing Earth and the number 4. Therefore the Lord is on Earth (4) and God is in Heaven (3). Since the Lord / God phenomenon seems to be pointing to this eternal concept of Heaven (3) and Earth (4), we should find a congruence between the numbers *Three* and *Four* and the words *Heaven* and *Earth*. And as it turns out, that is exactly what we find for both Heaven and Earth and Three and Four sum to **47**.

GOD (3)   THREE   HEAVEN
           7 6 5 5 5 = **28**   23 = 6 5 1 5 5 1
                          47
LORD [4]   FOUR   EARTH
           6 2 6 5 = **19**   24 = 5 1 5 7 6

The phrase "Do not take the Lord's name in vain" is really nothing more than saying "Do not take your own name in vain," for you are an aspect of the divine consciousness. In other words, don't devalue yourself. This also gives us a new understanding to the question, "Do you believe in God?" Understood correctly, this question is actually suggesting a much deeper inquiry. The real question is "Do you believe in yourself?"

GOD IS GOOD

Many priests and preachers throughout time have spoken about the glory of God and his works. We have been told of God's infinite intelligence and his undying love for mankind. God is said to live in every single moment and aspect of his creation. God is in fact, O**minpotent, O**mniscient and O**mnipresent. The big three O's. We have often been told that "God is Good" - could there be any way to prove this? Is it but a simple coincidence that the spelling of the word God is only a single O away from being "Good". Since God is said to work in mysterious ways, maybe we can utilize these three O's in G**o**d and G**oo**d and find an answer.

G**O**D
G**OO**D

OMNIPOTENT	OMNISCIENT	OMNIPRESENT	} **111**
2 1 1 53 2 7 5 1 7 = **34**	2 1 1 56 3 55 1 7 = **36**	2 1 1 53 5 56 5 1 7 = **41**	

The numerical equivalent of Omnipotent, Omniscient and Omnipresent sum to **111**. We will explore this number in depth later in the text, but for now, let's be creative with this ever-presence of God. If we understand that each 1 in 111 represents each O in our big three Os, uniting to represent the Holy Trinity, then we can combine these three Os and concentrate on the four letters that remain, G, G, D and D.

$$7 - G\text{O}D - 4$$
$$7 - G\text{OO}D - 4$$

By uniting the three Os and assigning the numerical equivalents for the G and D, we can find the number **22** $(7 + 7 + 4 + 4 = 22)$. Notice we have 7 letters in Good and God (Good: 4 and God: 3). The sum of the G, G, D and D (or 22) divided by the total number of letters (7) finds us Pi, 3.142.

$$7 - G\text{O}D - 4 \quad 7 + 7 + 4 + 4 = 22 / 7 = 3.142 \; \pi$$
$$7 - G\text{OO}D - 4 \quad G + G + D + D = 22 / \textbf{GOODGOD} = 3.142 \; \pi$$

The Omnipotence, omniscience and omnipresence of God are the recognition that his clever, playful, magical and poetic works are encoded in every-thing and in every moment. But most importantly, recognition of God is available to all who seek him. God asks only one thing of you and that is to be as he: clever, playful and poetic.

CHICKEN OR EGG?

The question of "What came first, the chicken or the egg?" is a truly profound philosophical question. Since an egg hatches a chicken and yet the chicken is needed to lay the egg, this simple question poses a unique paradox of thought. Where did it all start? Maybe our cipher can give us some clues.

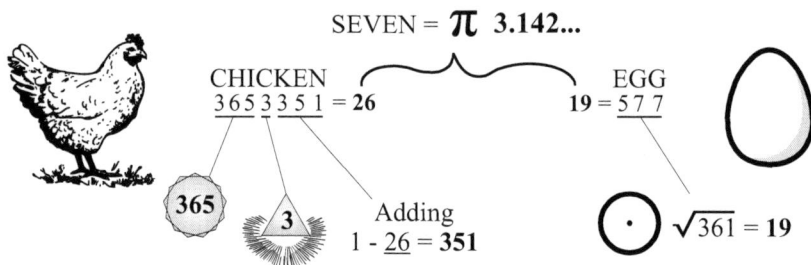

SEVEN = π 3.142...

CHICKEN
3 6 5 3 3 5 1 = 26

EGG
19 = 5 7 7

365

3

Adding
1 - 26 = 351

$\sqrt{361} = 19$

Chicken as it reads left to right, gives us three very important numbers: **365**, **3** and **351**. The first four numbers yield us the **365** days of the solar year, as well as our Holy Trinity of **3**. The last three numbers, or **351** is nothing more than adding the numbers 1 - 26 together, with the chicken itself summing to **26** representative of our alphabet, LordGod and the Hebraic Tetragrammaton. *Egg* sums to 19, a number we will explore in depth in the chapter "Genesis 1:1". 19 is the square root of the Greek Monad of 361. The Monad meant wholeness and divinity. Between the Egg and the Chicken is the 7 days of creation, which encodes in itself Pi.

Hinduism teaches the universe formed from an expanding egg called Brahmanda, a motif that we explored in Volume 1 with the primordial egg. How many animals lay eggs? Fish, birds, snakes, etc all do. The egg seems to be a fundamental archetype of nature herself, while the chicken is but one of the many forms crafted by the hands of time. So what came first, the chicken or the egg? Accordingly the answer is the egg. For even you first started out as an embryonic egg. Before you had ever felt the rays of the sun (**365**), before you had ever heard about the Holy Trinity (**3**) and before you had ever spoke the 26 letters of the alphabet (**351**), all of your potential was once encased inside an egg.

The egg leads us to the first moments of creation. It leads us to the very beginning of time itself. It leads us to the *other side* of pure, un-differentiated spirit - before the existence of existence itself. So the question, "Why did the chicken cross the road?" gives us a whole new insight into the answer: "To get to the *other side*."

15

THE EBONY AND IVORY OF PI

There are 88 keys on the standard grand piano representing 7 and 1/3 octaves, which is the range of sound that is the most comforting to our ears. We play these **88** keys with our two hands. Look down at your hands once again and count the number of phalanges on your fingers and thumbs. Each hand has four fingers with 3 phalanges each and a thumb with 2 phalanges making for a total of 14 phalanges with both hands, adding up to **28**.

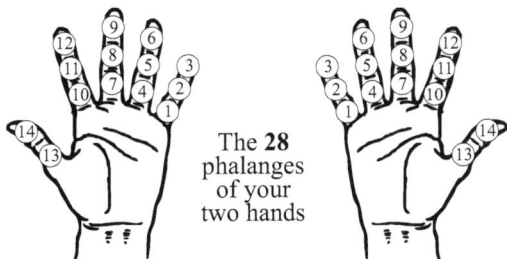

The **28** phalanges of your two hands

If we divide the number of keys on the grand piano, **88**, by the total sections of your two hands, **28**, we yield a whole number approximation of Pi.

88 keys / **28** sections of your two hands = π **3.142...**

Next time you bang away "Heart and Soul" on the **PI**ano with a friend, just remember that, not only are you making music, but you are also making Pi.

It takes **88** *keys* to make Pi. The word *key* yields us three different distinct associations. First, *key* in our cipher sums to 10, representing the 10 fingers of your two hands. Secondly, we know a *key* on the **PI**ano is the object in which you strike to create sound and compose a melody. Lastly, a *key* is also something you use to unlock or lock a door. The common denominator of these three keys *are your two hands*. The *key* is your 10 fingers, the *key*s on the piano beg you to create harmony and the *key* is to unlock the closed doors of your true potential. The universe is instructing you, in multiple ways, to find harmony in the self and create it in the world. It put the message right on your two hands.

16

KIDDING A "ROUND"

The Earth goes round the sun. The moon goes round the Earth. Our solar system goes round the galaxy. The stars spin round their central pole. Everything goes round and round and round in this great universe.

Following the cycles of time and the movement of the heavens was encoded into the much lost art of astrology. Astrological charts and calendars based on animal or anthropomorphic gods are found throughout the known world. In order to deeply understand the motions of the stars and planets, there is no doubt that one needs to know the power of the circle. Without looking no further than one's backyard, one can easily see the circular nature of nature: bird's nests, acorns, heads of flowers and tree trunks. Everything in the cosmos is spinning itself into existence. Whatever game the universe is playing, it is easy to see that it is most definitely kidding a*round.*

In the last volume, we correlated the numerical equivalent of *child* to the 365.24 day time span it takes the Earth to revolve around the Sun. This led us to the conclusion that we indeed must therefore be the Suns of God, for all of us were once children or a *child.* Another name for a child is *Kid.* Let's compare the numerical equivalents of these two adolescent names.

CHILD
3 6 52 4

KID
3 5 4

365.24 days /
12 months
of the Sun

354 days /
12 months
of the Moon

Notice *kid* gives us the numbers **354**. The synodic month, or the period of the Moon's phases, is a period of roughly 29.5 days (29.53 to be exact). If we correlate the 12 months of the solar year to 12 months of the lunar year, we find the numbers of the letters of *Kid* (12 x 29.5 = **354**). Beyond the wholeness of the eternal God exists the duality of our manifested reality. The power of both the sun and the moon, the grand opposites in our heavenly sky, exist within every *Child* and *Kid* on this great Earth.

"We dance round in a ring and suppose,
But the Secret sits in the middle and knows."
~ Robert Frost

17

AT PLAY WITH COLORED BALLS

The Greek philosopher Heraclitus said, "The Aeon is at play with colored balls." This philosophy, as well as the fundamental geometry of space itself, can be understood very simply through the art of juggling.

The word *juggling* derives from the Middle English *jogelen,* meaning to entertain by performing tricks. The art of juggling has been practiced for centuries now. The ancient wall painting shown above, discovered in the 15th tomb of the Karyssa I (c. 1994-1781 B.C.) in Egypt, clearly depicts juggling. Juggling is not only fun, but also a symbolic act that leads us to the geometry of creation. With one ball, the juggler can only toss it up or toss it between his hands. With two balls, the juggler can pass them back and forth or toss them up with each hand but still not too entertaining. It is only with three balls that one can commence juggling . The three balls needed to juggle echoes not only the Christian and Hindu Holy Trinities, but also one of the most consistently holy geometric symbols, the T*riangle,* (whose numerology sums to **33**!). One and two balls only create two points, but with three, there is plane and space for movement. A space created so you may entertain yourself and others.

There are **14** phalanges on each of your hands. If we assign the number **14** to each of our **3** juggling balls, that would give us three-fourteens (or **3 14**s) to work with in the art if juggling. Just like playing the piano, juggling finds us once again also making Pi. **3.14**

$$\pi$$
3.14
"Three - Fourteens"

SIX
$653 = 14$

The numerical equivalent of the word *Six* sums to **14**. Equating the three 14's to three *Six*es now gives us the number **666**.

THE UNITY OF OPPOSITES

Everything in nature has its opposite:

Man / Woman, Cold / Hot, Spirit / Matter, Wet / Dry, Right / Wrong,
Up / Down, Left / Right, Forward / Reverse

This Unity of Opposites is universally present in nature and is expressed on the human hands. Your left hand is a mirror of your right hand. We have used our hands as the key to understand music, mathematics, our alphabet and it has even led us to a deeper understanding of our freedom. Our hands come together in the act of prayer, unifying the left and the right to make ourselves whole. Since merging opposites is the intention of making oneself whole, we should therefore find the most wholly ratio of Pi when we merge opposites. And sure enough, Pi seems to have been hiding between opposites all of the time.

The numerical equivalent of *Difficult* equals **44** and *Easy* equals **14**. 44/14 = 3.142 or Pi. The message behind these two opposites seems to be a positive one. Apparently, whatever the hurdle may be, our language wants to remind us that it is "Easy as Pi."

$$\begin{array}{ll} \text{DIFFICULT} & \text{EASY} \\ 4\ 5\ 6\ 6\ 5\ 3\ 6\ 2\ 7 = \textbf{44} & 5\ 1\ 6\ 2 = \textbf{14} \end{array} \qquad 44 / 14 = \text{Easy as } \pi$$

The numerical equivalent of *On* equals **3** and *Off* equals **14**. Putting these two numbers together and placing a decimal point between them finds us the holy ratio of Pi once again.

$$\begin{array}{ll} \text{ON} & \text{OFF} \\ 2\ 1 = \textbf{3} & 2\ 6\ 6 = \textbf{14} \end{array} \qquad \text{ON} = \textbf{3 . 14} = \text{OFF}$$

Good and *Bad* are two extremes on one circular line. In order to find the truth within them both, one needs to unify these two polarities. Good and Bad combined equal 22 and Good and Bad combined have 7 letters. 22/7 = 3.142 or Pi. Lo and behold, combining these opposites finds us the transcendence of our wholly Pi.

$$\begin{array}{cc} \text{GOOD} & \text{BAD} \\ 7\ 2\ 2\ 4 & +\ 2\ 1\ 4 = \textbf{22} \end{array} \qquad 22 / 7 \text{ Letters} = \pi$$

The black and white keys on the piano represent the "major" and "minor" notes. *Major* sums to **13** and *Minor* sums to **14**. Mirroring these two numbers and placing the decimal after the mighty 3 we can once again find Pi lurking beneath the harmony, just waiting to be discovered.

$$\begin{array}{ll} \text{MAJOR} & \text{MINOR} \\ 1\ 1\ 4\ 2\ 5 = \textbf{13} & 1\ 5\ 1\ 2\ 5 = \textbf{14} \end{array} \qquad \boxed{13}\ \boxed{31}\ \&\ \boxed{14}\ \boxed{41} = \textbf{3.141 } \pi$$

ROLL YOUR BONES

The game of dice has been with us for quite some time. Dice have been used since before recorded history with the oldest known dice excavated as part of a 5000-year-old backgammon set at the Burnt City, an archeological site in south eastern Iran. Other excavations from ancient tombs in the Indus Valley civilization indicate a South Asian origin. Dicing is mentioned as an Indian game in the Rigveda, Atharvaveda and Buddha games list; it also plays a critical role in the great Hindu epic Mahabharata.

One dice is called a Die with its plural being Dice. The difference between Die and Dice is the ability to C, or our holy 3. *Die* sums to 14 and *Dice* sums to 17 with the difference being once again our Holy Trinity. The numerical equivalents of all six sides of the Die, *one*, *two*, *three*, *four*, *five* and *six* sum to **103**.

ONE	TWO	THREE	FOUR
2 1 5 = 8	7 4 2 = 13	7 6 5 5 5 = 28	6 2 6 5 =19

FIVE	SIX	
6 5 5 5 =21	6 5 3 = 14	**103**

Since one Die seems to be speaking about death, we should assume that the pair of Dice would give us life. *Dice* sums to 17. The numerical equivalent of *Game*, *Peace*, *Magic* and most importantly, *Live* all sum to 17 (another number we will explore in-depth in this text). With the numerical equivalents of the words *one* through *six* summing to **103**, that means a pair of dice would equal **206**. Not coincidentally, there are **206** bones in the *paradice* of the human body.

206 Bones

103   103

206

We can even find Pi in dice as well. The numbers *One* and *Six* are located on opposites sides of the die. *One* sums to **8** and *Six* sums to **14**. 14 + 8 = 22. 1 plus 6 equals 7. The numerical equivalents of the words divided by the sum of the numbers yields us Pi, 3.142.

How many people visit Las Vegas each year, try their hand at dice and have no idea the deep meaning hidden within? Next time you "roll your bones" the *game* of *dice* should now have a whole new meaning.

EIGHT DAYS A WEEK

The seven-day week is the standard week used by cultures the world over. Its origins most reflect the biblical creation story in Genesis. God manifested the world in six days and rested on the Sabbath creating a perfect framework for our 7 day week with Sunday, or the *day of the Sun*, being the holy day and day of rest. This 7-day week is the one encoded in the Aubrey Holes at Stonehenge, which follows the Lunar cycle of 4 weeks of 7 days, making a month 28 days and a year 13 months long. In the last volume, we discovered this calendar in the Mayan Pyramid at Chichen Itza, in the numerology of the deck of cards as well as in the numerical equivalents of both Jachin and Boaz (see Vol. 1, pp 40 - 41). Many of our ancient ancestors saw the universe as a symphony playing the grandest of songs. The Pythagoreans called this song "The Harmony of the Spheres" and envisioned the stars and planets dancing to the music of time. The perfect 5, 12, 13 Pythagorean triangle fits within the station stones and sections off the week according to the root to octave sequence of the major music scale - or 7 notes/days with the 8th day being the octave. By mapping the path of the Moon using a musical root to octave scale, our ancestors were in full recognition of the musical nature of our cosmos. By getting *in tune* with the universe, it gave the ancients the ability to find harmony within themselves.

Since Sunday is considered the most holy of days in many cultures, we can section off Sunday to Sunday on the adjacent end of our 5, 12, 13 triangle:

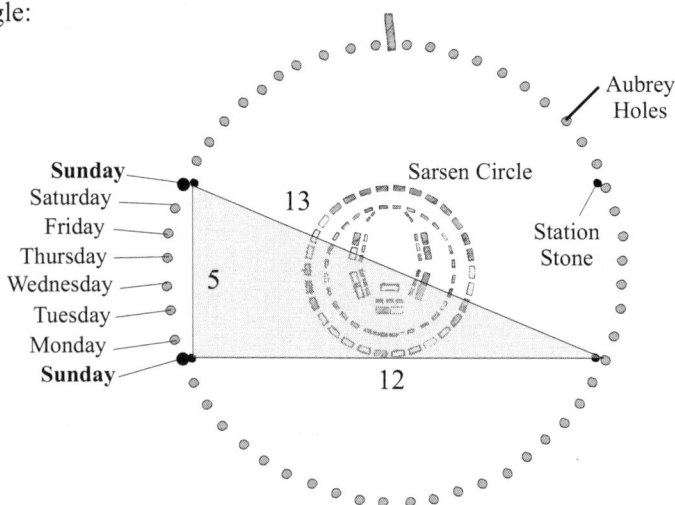

Using our cipher, the numerical equivalents of *Sunday* thru *Sunday* sums to **206,** directly reflecting the **206** bones in the human skeleton. This root to octave musical measure of the eight days of the week gives us a direct correlation between the bones of our human vessel and the intricate, magical workings of the hands of time. This numerical correspondence comes with a message: You are a *complete body of work,* perfectly crafted by time itself.

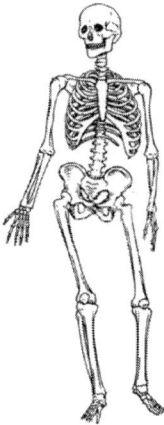

SUNDAY
6 6 1 4 1 2 = **20**

MONDAY
1 2 1 4 1 2 = **11**

TUESDAY
7 6 5 6 4 1 2 = **31**

WEDNESDAY
4 5 4 1 5 6 4 1 2 = **32**

THURSDAY
7 6 6 5 6 4 1 2 = **37**

FRIDAY
6 5 5 4 1 2 = **23**

SATURDAY
6 1 7 6 5 4 1 2 = **32**

SUNDAY
6 6 1 4 1 2 = **20**

Sunday to Sunday:
20 + 11 +
31 + 32 +
36 + 23 +
32 + 20 =
206

206
bones in the
Human skeleton

Interesting to note: If we remove one Sunday from our 8 days a week, giving us the traditional 7 days, this sums to **186**. The speed of light is measured at roughly **186**,000 miles per second (186,282 mps).

Modern science is currently searching for a Grand Unified Theory (GUT) or a Theory of Everything (TOE), but we do not wish to know merely the GUT or the TOE of the universe. What we yearn for is an understanding of *the complete body of work.* A fundamental bias exists in science that focuses less on deducing the essence of the human experience and more on inducing its own wild theories as to how the organized organism of this universe runs the show. To ignore and sometimes utterly disregard the viewpoint of the scientist who is conducting the experiment is absurd. The alchemists of old would say that placing man as a mere spectator in the grand cosmic drama is a fool's game. The only way to understand the universe is to first understand the tool it gave us to explore it: *the human vehicle.* In Volume 1 we learned of the cardinal rule of *gematria* or "coming up one short." By coming to know ourselves we can come to know this missing *one* and in doing so we might just be able to make sense of *the whole nine yards.*

THE ENNEAD

The Egyptians and the Greeks celebrated nine gods or principles called the Ennead and believed that these gods ruled the cosmos through the laws of number. The Christian angelic hierarchy, structured much like the Ennead, were 9 angels separated into 3 levels. These 9 gods led us to 9 numbers (1, 2, 3, 4, 5, 6, 7, 8, and 9), and those 9 led us to the world of decimals.

Decimal parity, or Kabbalistic Reduction, is the ancient numerological art of breaking down numbers to their decimal equivalent. For example, the number of the Monad, or 361, in decimal parity would be $3 + 6 + 1 = 10$ and $1 + 0 = 1$. Therefore, the essence or decimal parity reduction of 361 is One. This art is currently not accepted in modern mathematics. This numerological tool allows us to peer deeper into the many layers of numbers. Numbers are not merely symbols representing quantities, numbers are a language in and of itself that has much to say if we are willing to listen and be open to every way it wishes to speak to us. A few interesting measurements can be found by breaking our Ennead of 9 into a Trinity, 3 levels of 3 numbers each, reflective of the Christian angelic hierarchy:

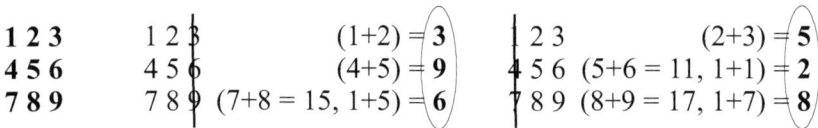

1 2 3	1 2 3	(1+2) = **3**	2 3 (2+3) = **5**
4 5 6	4 5 6	(4+5) = **9**	5 6 (5+6 = 11, 1+1) = **2**
7 8 9	7 8 9	(7+8 = 15, 1+5) = **6**	8 9 (8+9 = 17, 1+7) = **8**

Crossing off the 3, 6, and 9, adding the numbers across and breaking them down to their decimal parity equivalents gives us the number **396**. Multiply this by the next number in our number line, or 10, and we yield the radius of the Earth in miles, **3,960**. Crossing off the 1, 4, and 7 and doing the same to this Ennead yields us the number **528**. Multiply this by 10, and we yield the number of feet in an English Mile, **5,280**.

The decimal system (*deca* meaning Ten) utilizes the numbers 0, 1, 2 3, 4, 5, 6, 7, 8 and 9, or our Ennead and the placeholder 0 giving us *10 digits to work with*. When we count our apples, we start at 1, but when the universe counts its apples, it starts at *zero*. The zero is representative of the wholeness of our universe for it is indeed *our placeholder*. Intuiting the essences of the digits 0 - 9 may help us understand the cosmological principles that rule this world and quite possibly the worlds of beyond.

The sum of the addition of the numerical equivalents for zero - nine equals **180** (13 + 8 + 13 + 28 + 19 + 21 + 14 + 22 + 30 + 12 = **180**).

ZERO	ONE	TWO	THREE	FOUR	FIVE
1 5 5 2 =**13**	2 1 5 = **8**	7 4 2 = **13**	7 6 5 5 5 = **28**	6 2 6 5 =**19**	6 5 5 5 =**21**

SIX	SEVEN	EIGHT	NINE	$\left(\begin{array}{c}\text{TEN}\end{array}\right.$	
6 5 3 = **14**	6 5 5 5 1 = **22**	5 5 7 6 7 = **30**	1 5 1 5 = **12**	7 5 1 = **13** $\left.\right)$	

How interesting is it that the numerical equivalents of the first ten numbers formed in existence, or 0 - 9, sum to **180**, or the 180 degrees of half of a Pi?! The numerical equivalent of *Ten* sums to 13 and therefore, whether we use the digits 0 - 9 or 1 - 10 as our base ten system, the sum would equal 180! A very common glyph seen in Egypt is the semi-circle.

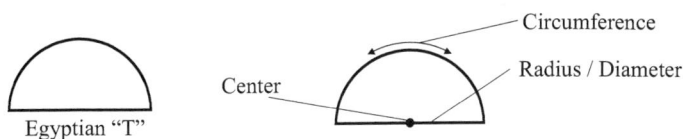

Egyptian "T" Center Circumference Radius / Diameter

This glyph encodes the power of 180 degrees. We can easily see that this symbol references the sun setting or rising on the horizon with the horizon becoming the diameter needed to find the circumference of the sun. We know that the word *Horizon* (equaling 22 and having 7 letters) encodes Pi, and this symbol also gave us some useful mathematical principles. This glyph is the letter **D** in the English alphabet but in the Egyptian alphabet it is the letter **T**. In linguistics, both the D and the T are what are considered dental consonants, or sounds made by the tongue making contact with the gum ridge. The T is also the symbol for the Tao Cross, a symbol meaning man and balance, and a mathematical principle adored by religions the world over. Our Ennead of 1 - 9 and our zero adding to 180 points to a cosmic truth embedded in the mathematics of creation: God's working with 9 numbers. *So what about that zero?*

It is well known that the Egyptians did not use a zero in their math, and this had led Egyptologists and mathematicians to the conclusion that the Egyptians must have been mistaken when making their calculations. What many fail to realize is that the Egyptians always considered zero, for *zero represented God*. It was the principle of the circle, the concept of all or nothing. It represented all that was, shall be, and is. The Omnipotent, Omniscient and Omnipresent. It could not be denied, and, therefore, we can assume that since this power of the circle was everywhere, it certainly didn't need to be written down, *for it was always **around**.*

The 180 degrees of our Ennead and zero can be found in the ancient mathematics of the Vedic peoples. The Vedas are a large body of sacred Hindu scriptures thousands of years old. The Hindu peoples of the past preferred to do their math around a circle and felt it best to keep it simple by using the 9 numbers of our Ennead. By placing **9** at the top, and putting the numbers around our circle, *encasing the zero*, we can draw an equilateral triangle, equaling **180** degrees, that connects the 3, 6, and 9. This 3, 6, and 9 are the end numbers in our Trinitarian breakdown of the Ennead, numbers that are divisible by a trinity as well as being the numbers the universe is founded upon according to Nikola Tesla, *"If you only knew the magnificence of the 3, 6, and 9, then you would have a key to the universe."*

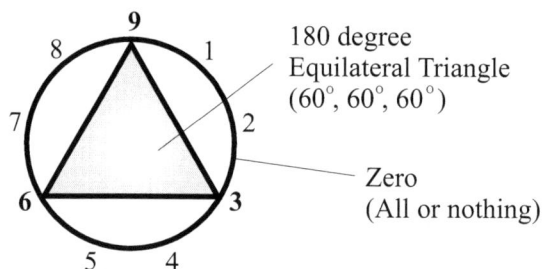

180 degree
Equilateral Triangle
$(60°, 60°, 60°)$

Zero
(All or nothing)

Not only does the numerical equivalent of zero through nine encode the 180 degrees of a triangle, but every single triangle you have ever seen does as well, for all internal angles of any triangle, no matter the shape or size, will equal **180 degrees**. This 180 degrees is signifying the initial split of our primordial egg of zero or 360 degrees. A cracked egg that *remains split but is indivisible*. The mighty triangle is the first geometric form in existence, for 1 and 2 are merely points on a graph, but when we find three we find connectivity, the first plane or space created as well our Ennead of 180 degrees.

Decimal parity allows us to take our first step down the pathway of the magical world of mathematics. It shows us the simplicity, eloquence and trickery the creator used when constructing the world. By being able to break down any number in the universe to 1 through 9, it allows us to understand our place in this circular world. For we exist in the decimal places anchored by that Mighty Trinity before the decimal point of Pi.

THE WHOLE NINE YARDS

Though the 12 inches of one foot is called an English foot, no one is sure where the this measurement originated. The English mathematician John Greaves, who extensively measured the Great Pyramid of Giza, found that the Egyptian builders used the English foot when constructing the pyramids. Seeing the importance in the measurement, Greaves decided to etch the length of the English Foot onto one of the pyramid's walls with the commandment "Let All Nations Obey." *Metrology*, or the study of measurement, was the key to the knowledge of God in the ancient world. The English foot, however it came into use, seems to have been built off the principles of 3, 6, and 9. Using decimal parity, we can reduce each English foot down to its decimal equivalent and find the equilateral triangle of 3, 6 and 9 embedded in the construction of this measure.

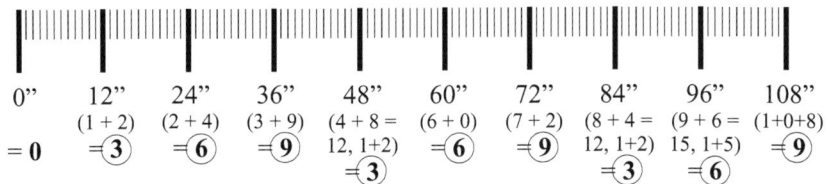

0"	12"	24"	36"	48"	60"	72"	84"	96"	108"
	(1 + 2)	(2 + 4)	(3 + 9)	(4 + 8 = 12, 1+2)	(6 + 0)	(7 + 2)	(8 + 4 = 12, 1+2)	(9 + 6 = 15, 1+5)	(1+0+8)
= 0	=3	=6	=9	=3	=6	=9	=3	=6	=9

Notice the 9th foot, or the highest angel in our Ennead hierarchy, equals **108** inches. We saw the power of the Holy 108 in the first volume and once again it shows its face in the Ennead of the English foot. The central pillar of our Holy 108 was the decimal reduction of the number 144. 12 English feet with 12 inches per foot equals **144**. It seems that the Grand Architect, when constructing infinity, had an affinity for certain numbers. Our ancestors recognized these holy numbers, encoded them into measure, and, to our blessing, passed them along to us.

The English foot and yard can be found in three perfect Pythagorean triangles. The basic 3, 4, 5 triangle is the most well-known and is the one most often used when teaching the Pythagorean formula ($a^2 + b^2 = c^2$) ($3^2 + 4^2 = 5^2$ or $9 + 16 = 25$). Adding up the sides of this triangle helps us determine the inches in the English foot ($3 + 4 + 5 = 12$). The shortest side, or the adjacent side, of this triangle represents the decimal reduction of our 12 inches down to 3.

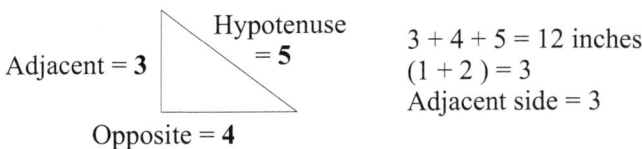

Adjacent = **3**
Hypotenuse = **5**
Opposite = **4**

$3 + 4 + 5 = 12$ inches
$(1 + 2) = 3$
Adjacent side = 3

26

We can double the first Pythagorean Triangle to find 2 feet (3, 4, 5 becomes 6, 8, 10). 6 + 8 + 10 = 24 inches with the adjacent being **6**. Now, by tripling the first 3, 4, 5 triangle, we can find our third foot of 36 inches: (3, 4, 5 becomes 9, 12, 15). 9 + 12 + 15 = 36 inches with the adjacent being **9**. This multiplication by 2 and by 3 is something we will revisit in our study of the Pythagorean Tetractys later in this text.

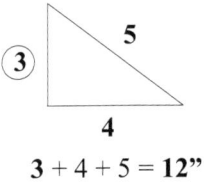

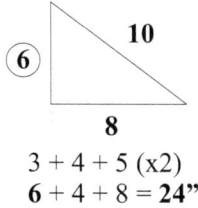

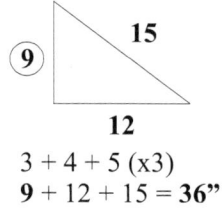

3 + 4 + 5 = **12"**

3 + 4 + 5 (x2)
6 + 4 + 8 = **24"**

3 + 4 + 5 (x3)
9 + 12 + 15 = **36"**

The 3, 4, 5 proportionate triangle is encoded into the Great Pyramid of Giza. By *squaring the circle*, the basic mathematical principle encoded in the Great Pyramid, a concept we will explore in depth in the next chapter, we can encase the moon on the Square of our Earth with our 3, 4, 5 triangle as shown below.

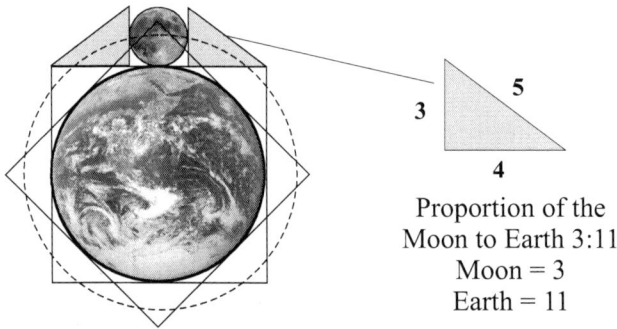

Proportion of the
Moon to Earth 3:11
Moon = 3
Earth = 11

The phrase *the whole nine yards* is a commonly used expression that means "the entirety of something", or "completion". Nine yards would be 324 inches (1 yard = 3 feet; 3 feet = 36 inches; 9 x 36 = 324). 324 is exactly 1 yard, or 3 feet, short of 360 inches. Why would the phrase "the whole nine yards" leave out one yard instead of making completion be 360, resonant with the 360 degrees of a circle? This 3 feet is representative of the three stages you will take through life: *childhood, middle age* and *old age*. These are the great steps, or phases, you will take to complete the circle of life. The whole nine yards is only complete if you count the person who is doing the counting. Only by *making yourself count* can you take the necessary steps to complete the journey of your life.

SQUARING THE CIRCLE

In the last volume we very briefly explored the ancient art of *squaring the circle* and how this ancient art, practiced by Hermeticists and alchemists alike, introduces a person to the measurements of the Earth and moon. We even saw how it helped put numbers to the letters of our alphabet using the Freemasonic symbol of a compass and square. The art of *squaring the circle* is shown again below.

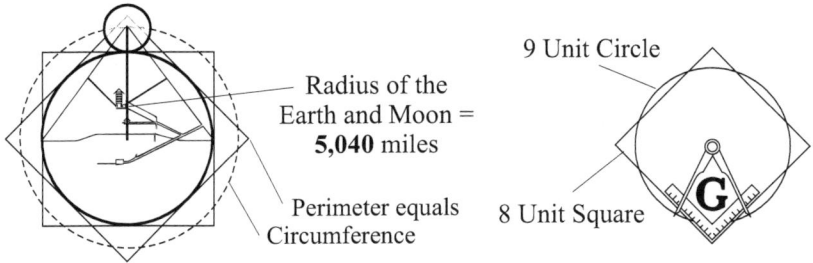

9 Unit Circle

Radius of the Earth and Moon = **5,040** miles

Perimeter equals Circumference

8 Unit Square

SQUARING THE CIRCLE
Circle of **9**: π x $4.5^2 \approx 63.63$
Square of **8**: $8^2 = 64$ $\cong$

One of the most notable wonders of the world, the Great Pyramid of Giza, squares the circle of the Earth to find us the combined radius of the moon and Earth to be 5,040 miles (as shown above). Not only does squaring the circle help us measure two of the most important cosmic bodies in our Solar System, but it also introduces us to mathematical concepts such as Pi and Phi and the Tao Cross (which we will explore later on in this text). The ratio of the Great Pyramid can be expressed in many different ways: 7:11, 14:22, 28:44, 56:88. A few of the mathematical gems encoded in the Great Pyramid are shown below:

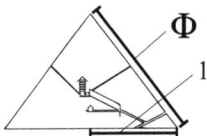

Φ
1
Radius of base = 1
Slope = 1.618

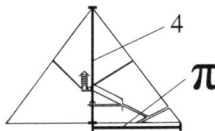

4
π
Height = 4
Radius of base = 3.141

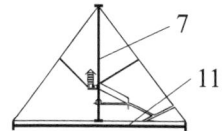

7
11
$1 \times 2 \times 3 \times 4 \times 5 \times 6 \times \underline{7} =$
5,040 Radius of Earth / Moon
$8 \times 9 \times 10 \times \underline{11} = $ **7,920**
Diameter of the Earth
(in miles)

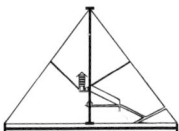

Base = 756 English Feet
Height = 480 English Feet
480 feet is 1/11 of a mile
Base / ½ Height (756 / 240) = **3.15**
3.15 - a close approximation of Pi
and the numbers of our Zodiac (see page 34)

28

The Great Pyramid of Giza remains a mystery. Millions of stones, weighing multiple tons each, were used to construct this modern day engineering nightmare. However the Egyptians constructed this magnificent piece of architecture, it can not be surpassed today. So many questions surround this pyramid: How was it built? What was it built for? How did a supposed post-stone age culture build something of such magnitude? The Egyptians made the Great Pyramid of Giza earthquake proof, hence, whatever it was built for, the architects wanted its message to last throughout the ages. Through the harsh winds of the sands of time, the Great Pyramid of Giza still stands begging us to solve its riddle.

The internal angles of the Great Pyramid of Giza will be important to focus on to help us understand much of what the Great Pyramid of Giza is trying to tell us.

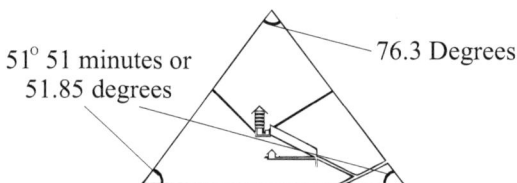

51° 51 minutes or 51.85 degrees

76.3 Degrees

The bottom two angles on the pyramid are roughly 51.85 degrees. This is also expressed in arc minutes as **51** degrees, **51** minutes. This **51** became important in correlating many terms that sum to **51** and reference divinity.

Tetragrammaton, Lost Masonic Word, Isis/Osiris, Philosophers, Universal Panacea, Elixir of Life, Metatron's Cube, Trestleboard, Supreme Being, Circumambulation

When *squaring the circle*, we find the radii and, thus, the diameters of both the Earth and the moon. When we do this, we can find a whole number ratio for these two heavenly bodies. When one draws a circle with a diameter equal to **3** and a circle with a diameter equal to **11**, this is a very close approximation of the Moon to Earth ratio. Using our cipher, *Three* equals 28 and *Eleven* equals 23, together summing to **51**.

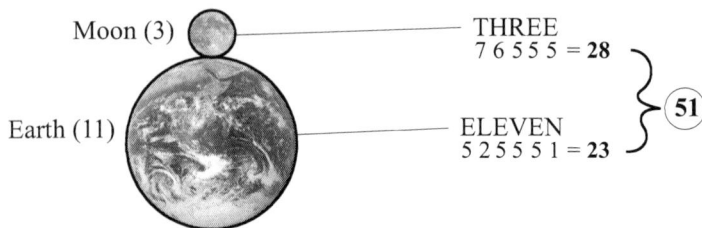

Moon (3)

Earth (11)

THREE
7 6 5 5 5 = **28**

ELEVEN
5 2 5 5 5 1 = 23

51

As we know, all interior angles of a triangle will add up to 180 degrees. With the bottom two angles being 51.85, this would leave the apex or peak of the Great Pyramid of Giza to be 76.3 degrees (51.85 x 2 = 103.7, 180 degrees - 103.7 = **76**.3). If we round these degrees to their nearest whole number, we find the missing capstone of the Great Pyramid to be **76** degrees. This angle pointing towards the heavens is important because it is the only angle that the Great Pyramid builders did not give us, since there is no capstone. By not giving us this **76** degrees, the builders of the Great Pyramid of Giza were asking us to participate in finishing the Pyramid. The mystery of the missing capstone would have to be pursued through the study of mathematics. Only by *squaring the circle* can we find our missing **76**.

SQUARING THE CIRCLE
6 4 6 15517 7 65 355 3 25 = **76**

There is little doubt that the Egyptians were skilled craftsman, masons, architects, mathematicians and astronomers. The Egyptians left behind proof in stone that they had reached a high level of consciousness, had a deep and intuitive understanding of this world (and the next), and were able to do magical things that would seem unheard of in today's world. They were master geometers or Earth-measurers, mapped the Heavens above and mapped the heaven within the human being. In order to align their pyramids to the heavens and then align the heavens to themselves, they would have to have an intimate knowledge of both *Longitude* and *Latitude*.

LONGITUDE   LATITUDE
2 2 1 757 6 4 5 + 2 1 757 6 4 5 = **76**

One of the most heavily used symbols throughout Hermeticism, alchemy and Freemasonry is *The Eye of Providence,* also known as the All-Seeing Eye of God. As seen on the back of the U.S. one dollar bill, this cryptic symbol is a pyramid with an eye in the middle of the capstone, elevated with a radiant glow of light shining directly behind it. This symbol is and has been used time and time again by occultists, in various organizations and even in many advertising campaigns. It is a powerful symbol with deep roots and pregnant with meaning.

All Seeing-Eye of God   The Eye of Providence

30

In leaving the mathematical problem of *squaring the circle* unfinished the Egyptians were asking for our hands in solving the puzzle. This riddle in stone and the symbolism surrounding it reminds us that the symbol of the *eye* is also the symbol of the *I*. The alchemists of the past knew of the inter-connectedness of everything in the universe and realized that this wholeness was not only divine but also a collective singular consciousness, or in other words, *God is an I*. God is looking at his creation, and he is using your eyes to do it. Every *I* is an *eye* of God. You are indeed the *All-Seeing Eye of God* for you are, in fact, *The Eye of Providence*.

THE EYE OF PROVIDENCE   ALL SEEING EYE OF GOD
7 6 5   5 2 5   2 6   3 5 2 5 5 4 5 1 3 5 = **76** | **67** = 1 2 2   6 5 5 5 1 7   5 2 5   2 6   7 2 4

In order to realize this cosmic truth, one must learn to speak the language that God speaks: mathematics. The foundation of the entire universe rests on simple mathematical laws. This is why our ancestors focused so much on geometry and number and deemed them *sacred*. Mathematics was a map to help find the path to the top of the grandest pyramid of all; *the universe within man*.

In our chapter entitled "The Cipher", we looked at putting the alefbet, or the first two letters in the Hebrew alphabet onto our two hands to find ourselves to be the *Master of the House*.

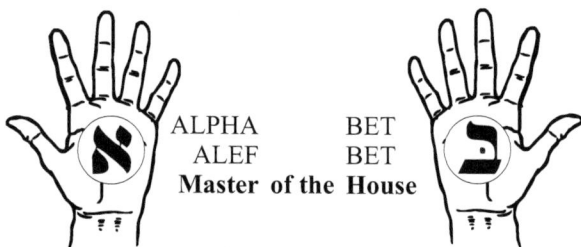

ALPHA   BET
ALEF   BET
Master of the House

MASTER OF THE HOUSE   KEEPER OF THE BALANCE
1 1 6 7 5 5   2 6   7 6 5 6   2 6 6 5 = **76** | **67** = 3 5 5 3 5 5   2 6   7 6 5 2 1 2 1 1 3 5

Like *The Eye of Providence*, the numerical equivalent of *Master of the House* confirms our place as masters of our own existence. In the Book of the Dead, the Egyptians refer to a deity called the "Keeper of the Balance." Since our hands are symmetrical, or reflections of each other, we can consider them as equals or *balanced*. With this assessment, maybe we can get a better understanding of just who this God is that the Egyptians may have been referring to. Maybe we have to look no further than down at our own two hands to see the supreme balance of God.

31

DOUBLING THE CUBE

Much like *squaring the circle, doubling the cube* was considered one of the most important mathematical problems to the ancients. The problem arose by needing to find the volume of a cube that was exactly double the size of the original. At first this may seem like an easy task, for if we wish to double something, it seems that all we would need to do is multiply by 2, but the solution is not that easy. The problem can be solved using basic algebra. If the original cube has a side S long its volume will be S^3. Therefore, a cube with double the volume of this cube is equal to $2S^3$ So one side of the new cube will equal:

DOUBLING THE CUBE

$$(2S^3) = S\sqrt[3]{2} = S \times 1.26$$

Cube with Sides equal to 1

1.26

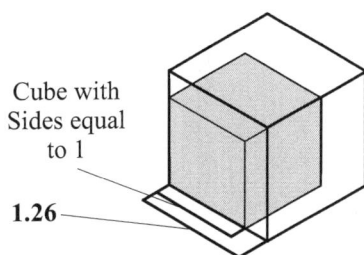

To make things simple, we can focus on this number **1.26**, the key number needed to double the cube. Multiply each side of a cube by this number and you will find its double. This number becomes very important in understanding the numerical breakdown of *doubling the cube.*

DOUBLING THE CUBE
4 2 6 2 2 5 1 7 7 6 5 3 6 2 5 = **63**

Doubling the cube sums to **63**. If we *double this number* we end up with our key digits or **126** (63 x 2 = 126). In Volume 1 we saw that the decimal parity equivalent of the 12 ages of the zodiac equaled **63** as did the 33rd and highest degree of Scottish Rite Freemasonry, or the *Inspector General*, shown again below.

The Numerical Equivalent and Decimal Parity Reduction
of the 12 Houses of the Zodiac

Aquarius = 34 **(7)**, Capricorn = 28 **(1)**, Sagittarius = 56 **(2)**,
Scorpio = 26 **(8)**, Libra = 24 **(6)**, Virgo = 15 **(6)**, Leo = **9**, Cancer = 18 **(9)**,
Gemini = 24 **(6)**, Taurus = 31 **(4)**, Aries = 22 **(4)** and Pisces = 28 **(1)**
Decimal Parity: **7 + 1 + 2 + 8 + 6 + 6 + 9 + 9 + 6 + 4 + 4 + 1 = (63)**

33rd INSPECTOR GENERAL
5 1 6 3 5 3 7 2 5 7 5 1 5 5 1 2 = **63**

The Freemasons communicate with each other through the art of secret phrases, symbols and handshakes. One very cryptic phrase shared by the brotherhood is *"Are you a traveling man?"* This phrase is of course highly symbolic. The travels that the Freemason is asking about is the travels one takes into the depths of his own being, in search of knowledge and the light of truth. It is a question about one's own passion and commitment to pursuing one's higher self. Getting yourself in order was directly related to finding order in this universe. This order is and always has been found in number. Geometry and metrology are of the utmost importance to the Freemasons. Understanding mathematical principles such as doubling the cube allows one a deeper understanding of the workings of the Grand Architect. Like *doubling the cube, "Are you a traveling man?"* sums to **63** as well.

ARE YOU A TRAVELING MAN?
1 55 2 2 6 1 7 5 1 5 5 2 51 7 1 1 1 = **63**

The cube is one of the 5 Platonic solids, which are considered by the alchemists and the neo-platonists to be the fundamental geometric forms at work in the universe. The cube also encodes the sacred geometrical seed of life, as well as the six directions of space and the axis upon which you sit.

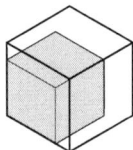

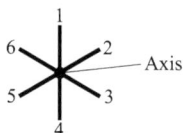

Seed of Life

The Kabaa, or Cube located in Mecca, Saudi Arabia is the most sacred site in all of Islam. According to the Koran, the cube was said to have been built by Abraham and his son Ishmael. Muslims pray towards the Kabaa and are required to make the Hajj pilgrimage at least once in his or her lifetime. Muslims walk 7 times around the cube called the *tawaf* a process known as *circumambulation* which equals **51**, the same as the *Tetragrammaton*. At times, 6 million people gather together for the Hajj to *circle the square* of this great cube of God.

Circling the Square

33

Our key number in the art of *doubling the cube* is **1.26**. Since we *doubled* the numerical equivalent of *doubling the cube*, or **63**, to find our **126**, let's *halve* our *doubling the cube* to see what it has to offer.

DOUBLING THE CUBE
4 2 6 2 2 5 1 7 7 6 5 3 6 2 5 = 63   **63 / 2 = 31.5**

We found our number **63** in the decimal parity equivalent of the 12 houses of the Zodiac. Using regular addition on the Zodiac, we also find the digits of *half* of our *doubling the cube* or **315**.

Aquarius = **34**, Capricorn = **28**, Sagittarius = **56**,
Scorpio = **26**, Libra = **24**, Virgo = **15**, Leo = **9**, Cancer = **18**,
Gemini = **24** , Taurus = **31**, Aries = **22** and Pisces = **28**
34 + 28 + 56 + 26 + 24 + 15 + 9 + 18 + 24 + 31 + 22 + 28 = **315**

This number must be noted, as this is not the first time we have seen the digits **315**. We also saw these same digits in the dimensions of the Great Pyramid of Giza.

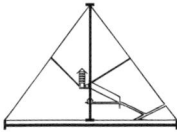

Base = 756 English Feet
Height = 480 English Feet
480 feet is 1/11 of a mile
Base / ½ Height (756 / 240) = **3.15**
3.15 - a close approximation of Pi

The base of the Great Pyramid divided by half its height equals **3.15**. This **3.15** is only .01 off from that holy ratio of Pi. The digits **315** resonate with not only our zodiacal cycle but also with halving the numerical equivalent of *doubling the cube*. It is truly remarkable how even inside the rigid corners of the cube, Pi seems to be lurking, just a decimal away from being found.

The Great Pyramid of Giza is a doorway into the archetypal architecture of the cosmic order. The Egyptians understood that the framework of God's holy word was fundamentally numerical and geometric. Counting the pedals of any flower can help one see this simple truth. *Squaring the circle* and *doubling the cube* are simple mathematical problems that initiate one into a world of dimension, proportion, geometry, measure, symbol, and, ultimately, pure beauty. And as the poet George Keats reminded us, "Beauty is truth, truth beauty." There is a mystery, a beauty and ultimately *an answer* in number. If the pyramids are trying to tell us anything, mathematics is the language they're speaking.

NUMBERS AND LETTERS

The phrase *In Hoc Signo Vinces* shown on the insignia above means "In this sign you will conquer." It was passed down to us from Greek to Latin, was used heavily by the Knight's Templar and remains a prominent Freemasonic phrase today. Interestingly, *In Hoc Signo Vinces* sums to **63**, the numerical equivalent of the 33rd and highest degree of Freemasonry, the *Inspector General*.

INSPECTOR GENERAL
5 1 6 3 5 3 7 2 5 7 5 1 5 5 1 2 = **63**

IN HOC SIGNO VINCES
5 1 6 2 3 6 5 7 1 2 5 5 1 3 5 6 = **63**

According to legend, Constantine I adopted the motto after his vision of a Chi Rho in the sky just before the Battle of Milvian Bridge against Maxentius, October 312. The early Christian symbol consists of a monogram composed of the Greek letters *Chi* (**X**) and *Rho* (**P**), the first two letters in the name Christ (Xpistos). Using our cipher, the elements attributed to Christ, the *Chi Rho* and **XP** find us the most interesting sacred mathematical principles and numbers. The letters **X** and **P** in our cipher both equal 3, together representing the 33 years of Christ's life and the 33 degrees of Freemasonic ascension. X and P added together sums to 6 representative of the 6 dimensions of space as shown on the picture of the Chi Rho below. Chi in our cipher finds us the numbers 365, or the 365 days of our solar year. Chi sums to 14 and Rho sums to 13, combining to give us our all-important, never-tiring, holiest of holy ratios, **3.141**. (Chi) 14 + (Rho) 13 = **27**, and this **27** finds us *Jesus,* the *Light,* and the *Lamb of God.*

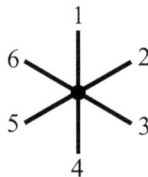

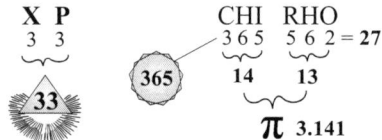

X P
3 3

CHI RHO
3 6 5 5 6 2 = **27**
14   13
π 3.141

365

33

JESUS
4 5 6 6 6 = **27**

LIGHT
2 5 7 6 7 = **27**

LAMB OF GOD
2 1 1 2 2 6 7 2 4 = **27**

The anthropomorphized sun of God, or the *Light,* deemed Christ was known as the *Christos* in Greek and *Khrisna* in Hinduism. This Christos figure was an archetype used again and again, in culture after culture, and it represented the ascended spirit of the reborn man. This *Christ* is the *Adam Kadmon* in Jewish mysticism, the *Hermes Trismegistus* and *Thoth* of Greece and Egypt, the *Buddha* in Buddhism and the *Hiram Abiff* in Freemasonry. This archetypal figure represented the graceful, wise and loving human that lay dormant within every single being. Christ means "anointed one" and is derived from the word *chrism* meaning "oil mingled with balm." This oil is also known by the alchemists as the Elixir of Life and represented the spinal fluid that traveled up the **33** bones of one's spinal column illuminating the 7 chakras or wheels in the endocrine system, known as raising the Kundalini serpent. The raising of this fluid, through good practice primarily balance, passion, commitment, meditation and study is the path one needs to take to achieve enlightenment. *It is the one and only path* that is individualized for each individual. You and only you can find your way. The zen and occult masters, divinatory practices and wise books of old may surely help you along, *but the path you must take is your own.* This path to enlightenment is known as Christhood, the Great Work, the Hero's Journey, the Mystic Quest and the Way or the Tao. Once the oil has ascended high enough into the brain it enters the pineal gland and illuminates dormant brain cells, allowing the ascended master to *see the light.* This oil is also sometimes referred to as a stone with the alchemical Philosopher's Stone and the Lapis being direct references. The oil traveling up the 33 bones of the *spinal column* and illuminating the *pineal gland* gives us both the 32 and 33 degrees of Freemasonry.

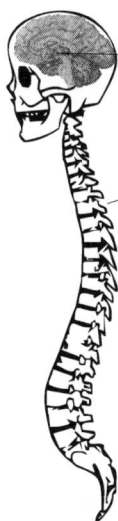

PINEAL GLAND
3 5 1 5 1 2 7 2 1 1 4 = **32**

SPINAL COLUMN
6 3 5 1 1 2 3 2 2 6 1 1 = **33**

The 33 years of Jesus' life and the 33 miracles he performed are direct numerical references to the path of enlightenment, understood by the 33 bones of the spine. The 18 years missing in the account of Jesus' life are symbolic of the years Jesus went searching for the God within. Once the fluid, or Christ, ascended into his pineal body, Jesus assumed a new distinction. Jesus *was* Jesus of Nazareth. *He became the Christ.*

This ascension has been symbolized in numerous ways throughout history; anytime a ladder, staff, scepter, wand or rod is depicted in mythology, it is most assuredly a reference to the spinal column and the oil or chrism that flows within it. The Rod of Asclepius, Staff of Hermes and Cadeceus are all references to this alchemical process and this physiological process is at the heart of religions worldwide. In order to complete the alchemical work, a study of the self and of the cosmos must be undertaken. One must measure himself against the cosmos and find his place in it. Luckily for us, the universe gives us some handy tools to do this work, mainly *numbers*, *letters* and those Freemasonic tools of the square and compasses.

Jesus, being a carpenter, was obviously well acquainted with the compass and square. These simple tools allow one to easily measure the cosmos as we have seen with squaring the circle. The 33rd degrees that Jesus climbed are recognized within the Earth. The Earth vibrates at 7.83 hertz due to lightning discharges called the Schumann resonance. The human scale resonants at 33 harmonics or overtones above this frequency or the range where in humans hear. We also find the 33 degrees of Freemasonry when we find Pi on the Earth. Making the diameter of the Earth a unit of 20 would make the circumference of the Earth roughly equal to **63** (20 x 3.142 = 62.84 or rounded up to **63**), once again the numerical equivalent of *Inspector General* and *In Hoc Signo Vinces*.

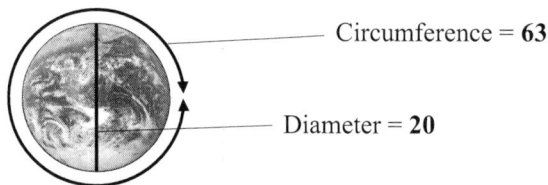

Circumference = **63**

Diameter = **20**

The *archetypal* character of Jesus, or the wise ascended master, is he who mastered all aspects of knowledge: writing, astrology, mathematics, geometry, etc. Jesus' ability to tell symbolic parables that encoded the cosmological principles showed his mastery of all crafts. Jesus was in full realization that he was a divine aspect of the great word or logos of God. Jesus was a 33rd degree Freemason, an *Inspector General* and was a master craftsman with both *Letters* and *Numbers*.

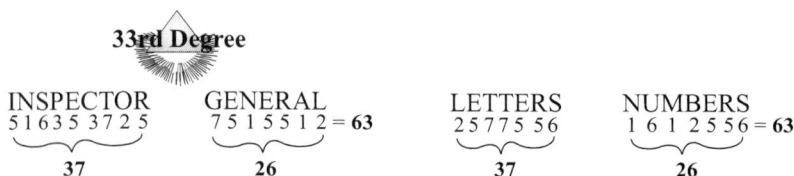

33rd Degree

INSPECTOR	GENERAL	LETTERS	NUMBERS
5 1 6 3 5 3 7 2 5	7 5 1 5 5 1 2 = **63**	2 5 7 7 5 56	1 6 1 2 5 56 = **63**
37	26	37	26

37

THE TAU CROSS

The symbol τ was used in mathematics to represent the Golden Ratio until the Greek letter *Phi* (Φ) gained prominence (after the first letter of Phidias, acclaimed sculptor of the Parthenon). Tau is also known as the symbol representing the ratio of any circle's circumference to its radius (equal to 2π).

A circle is defined as all points in a plane a certain radius away from a center point. The unit circle has a radius of 1, not a diameter of 1. Angles measured in radians make more sense using τ rather than 2π because τ radians measure a full circle, so 1/4 circle is τ/4, 1/2 circle is τ/2 and so on.

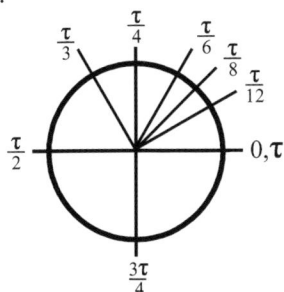

$T\tau$ The Greek letter Tau

τ Tau vs. π Pi
Example:
π / 2 becomes τ / 4
π / 4 becomes τ / 8 etc.

The Tau Cross is undoubtedly a symbol for man. The cross in mythology has often been a metaphor for the cross of matter, a symbol for the human vessel - where the spirit or energy source resides or where it is *nailed* to. The *spiritual* being of Jesus on the cross is a direct reference to this occult truth. Notice the Greek letter of the Tau Cross is much like that of Pi, given rise to the notion that Pi must be intrinsically connected to man.

π Pi τ Tau, the Cross of Man

The numerical equivalents for the Tau Cross, as we will see, leads us right back to Egypt, the birthplace and home of the masters of the alchemical arts as well as to the halls of the Freemasons. The sum of *Tau* equals **14** and *Cross* sums to **22**.

TAU CROSS
7 1 6 = **14** 3 5 2 6 6 = **22**

The Great Pyramid of Giza has a ratio of 14:22, the base being 22 and its height being 14. Not only do the two numbers that we get from the Tau Cross point directly to the Great Pyramid as well as to the symbol of a **T**, (the two lines needed to find the ratio), but the multiplication of these two numbers does as well. In the chapter on *squaring the circle* we established that the bottom two angles of the Great Pyramid measured 51.85 degrees. Rounding this number up reveals both of these angles to be 52 degrees. The multiplication of the numerical equivalent of *Tau*, or **14**, times the numerical equivalent of *Cross* or **22**, yields us the number **308** (14 x 22 = **308**). 360 degrees minus the 52 degrees of our bottom angles, measure **308** degrees.

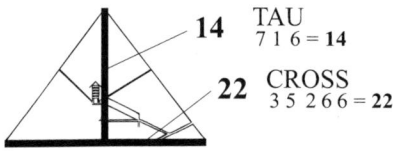

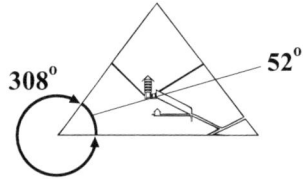

The simple geometric arrangement of these two lines coming together says much about the construction of our world. The standard cross itself is nothing more than these same two lines coming together except resting on each others centers. The depth of information about the fundamental mathematical structure of our reality that one can extract from two simple lines is quite remarkable and says much about our creator. Is our world too complicated to understand or have we over-intellectualized something that, at the heart, is profoundly simple? Leonardo Da Vinci wanted to tell us about the beauty of this cross in *The Vitruvian Man*. Put your feet together and extend your arms and you will find this magical Tau Cross *within you*.

These two lines, one *Vertical*, symbolizing spiritual ascension, and one *Horizontal*, symbolizing the material form, also point us to the 32 and 33 degrees of Scottish Rite Freemasonry.

HORIZONTAL   VERTICAL
6 2 5 5 1 2 1 7 1 2 = **32**   5 5 5 7 5 3 1 2 = **33**

PHYLLOHARMONY

Phyllotaxis is the degree at which leaves will arrange themselves around a plant to receive the optimal light and rain. This leaf arrangement is one of the wonders of the natural world, for it shows the simple and elegant intelligence within mother nature. This degree is based on the Fibonacci Sequence, or the ratio of Phi, 1.618. This angle the leaves grow into measures **137.5** degrees. The original Freemasonic compass was opened to 47 degrees, and the square gives us the 90 degrees of a right angle. Adding the degrees of the compass and square would yield us the number **137** (47 + 90 = 137). This is a mere .5 degrees off from the degree to which much of the botanical kingdom grows.

Phyllotaxis -
Leaf arrangement
137.5 Degrees of Phi

137.5°

47 degrees

90 degrees

A whole number approximation of Pi was widely known in the past by dividing **864** by 275 (864 / 275 = 3.142). The number **864** is important for the numerology of Jesus (27) multiplied by Christ (32) equals **864,** and the diameter of the sun measures **864,**000 miles. The radius of the Sun would therefore be **432,**000 miles. **432** x **432** = 186,642, a close approximation of the speed of light. The natural world seems to resonate within the range of **432** hertz. Beautiful, complex geometrical forms arise in the science of cymatics when **432** hertz is used. The original Stradivarius violin was tuned to **432** hertz. At the sacred Mount Meru in Tanzania, there are **432** Buddha Statues. The degree of Phyllotaxis multiplied by Pi (3.142) sums to **432.**025 or rounded down to the whole number **432** (137.5 x 3.142 = 432.025). Or better stated, Phyllotaxis x Pi = Harmony.

137 is the **33**rd prime number (resonate with the **33** degrees of Free-masonry) and shows its face in the world of quantum physics as well. The *fine structure constant* is a dimension-less physical constant widely used in particle physics when trying to understand the motion of electrons around atoms, approximated with the number **137** (the reciprocal of 1/137). Interesting to note, this number is .000000000000000000000000000000 000663, having **33** zeroes. **137** with **33** zeroes and **137** being the **33**rd prime number? Could this all be coincidence or is there perchance an underlying, *harmonic* order within the Godly world of numbers?

SPIRIT AND MATTER

To many of the occultists, *Spirit* (sometimes interpreted as consciousness) and **M**atter are considered not to be independent realities, but rather two facets or aspects of the absolute reality. *Spirit* is the energy source that is derived from the higher spheres of existence and *Matter* is the objective lower plane to which spirit resides. These two poles create the unity of all-being to which many ancient traditions saw as mainly a temporary illusion or hologram often deemed *Maya*. According to the Greek philosopher Protagoras, "Man is a measure of all things", and henceforth the human body should be a perfect measure of the unification of spirit and matter. Using our cipher *Spirit* sums to 31 and *Matter* sums to 26 together equaling **57**. Using decimal parity on our numbers reveals two numbers **4** and **8**. If we do the numerical equivalents for the number *Fifty Seven* it as well gives us the numbers **4** and **8**.

$$\text{SPIRIT} \quad \text{MATTER} \quad\quad\quad \text{FIFTY} \quad \text{SEVEN}$$
$$635557 + 1\ 17\ 755 = 57 \quad\quad 65672 \quad 6\ 5\ 5\ 5\ 1 = \boxed{48}$$
$$31 \quad\quad 26 \quad\quad\quad\quad 26 \quad\quad 22$$
$$3 + 1 = \boxed{4} \quad 2 + 6 = \boxed{8} \quad\quad 2 + 6 = \boxed{8} \quad 2 + 2 = \boxed{4}$$

Counting the sections of one's toes and hands, 14 for each hand and 10 for each foot, gives us 24 for our left hand and foot and 24 for our right hand and foot, together totaling **48** - informing us that we are indeed the perfected unity of both spirit and matter. 48 is also the number of hours in two days - 24 for the moon and 24 the sun, once again reflective of opposites of spirit (sun) and matter (moon).

The mirror of **57** is **75**. The first 75 digits of Pi sum to 360, representing the 360 degrees of the unity consciousness.

3. + 1 + 4 + 1 + 5 + 9 + 2 + 6 + 5 + 3 + 5 + 8 + 9 + 7 + 9 + 3 + 2 + 3 + 8 + 4 + 6 + 2 + 6 + 4 + 3 + 3 + 8 + 3 + 2 + 7 + 9 + 5 + 0 + 2 + 8 + 8 + 4 + 1 + 9 + 7 + 1 + 6 + 9 + 3 + 9 + 9 + 3 + 7 + 5 + 1 + 0 + 5 + 8 + 2 + 0 + 9 + 7 + 4 + 9 + 4 + 4 + 5 + 9 + 2 + 3 + 0 + 7 + 8 + 1 + 6 + 4 + 0 + 6 + 2 + 8 = **360**

Also notice 75% is the fraction 3/4 or Heaven (3) over Earth (4).

And last but not least, **57** in a base seven system (an idea we will cover later in the chapter "Genesis 1:1") equals **111**, once again representing the unity of all consciousness (*Omnipotent, Omniscient, Omnipresent*). Adding the first 23 numbers (or 23 representing *Heaven*) of Pi together also sums to **111**. Go ahead and find Heaven yourself. *Do the math.*

THE GREAT PI IN THE SKY

Our mighty sun courses through the sky throughout the year and forms what is called in astronomy an *Analemma* - Greek for "pedestal of a sundial." The analemma is the curve representing its changing angular offset from its mean position as viewed from our mother Earth. Because of the Earth's annual revolution around the sun in an orbit that is elliptical and tilted relative to the plane of the equator, an observer on Earth sees the Sun appear to move in an analemma around a mean position, taking a year to do so. If the sun is plotted (which can easily be done with a sundial and hence its name) or photographed at the same time every day, it will form a figure **8** as shown below:

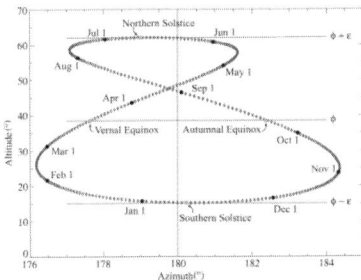

Analemma plotted at Noon, Royal Observatory, Greenwich

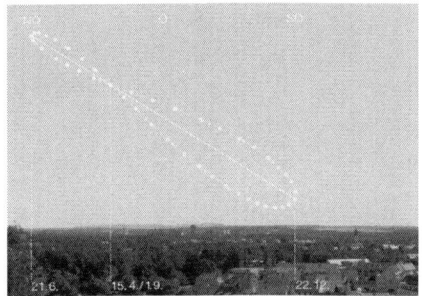

Like so many important words in our cipher such as *God, Lord* and *Psalm*, our *Sun* sums to **13**. Since the sun is the source of our light, *Lord*ing over us in its *God*ly manner, it should be no surprise that the path it takes, or its *analemma* sums to this all-important **13** as well.

SUN	ANALEMMA
6 6 1 = 13	1 1 1 2 5 1 1 1 = 13

In Volume 1 we discussed the fact that as the sun sets, the horizon can actually be used as the diameter to find the circumference of the sun, giving us a direct mathematical reference to the *Great Pi in our Sky*. We know Pi in our cipher actually sums to **8**, and this figure **8** the sun makes in the sky makes perfect sense of the numerology of our holy ratio. Not only does this figure 8 record the path of the sun throughout our year, but it also speaks of the infinite nature of the cycles of our universe, for we know the **8** is nothing more than the infinity sign stood upright. The Great Eight, or Pi in our Sky, through its movements has a symbolic message it wants to share with us of the infinite, boundless nature of its eternal spiritual fire. The life-giving force of our sun gave you a temporary life in the infinitude of time. Follow its path to find the light within you, and it will direct you to your true immortal nature.

THE BIG APPLE

Sir Isaac Newton, when explaining to someone how he came up with his theory of gravity, exclaimed that an apple had fallen from a tree and knocked him on his head. Is it possible that Newton never intended this story to be an actual account of how he came to understand the laws of gravity? Netwon was a practicing alchemist and there should be no doubt that this story has a much deeper symbolic significance. Mythologically, the apple is attributed to be the forbidden fruit eaten by Adam and Eve in the Garden of Eden. We've also been told that eating one once a day will keep the doctor away. What is so important about the apple?

The apple is representative of the toroidal shape of our galaxy, a pattern expressed in numinous ways throughout nature. As shown below, the stem and bottom of the apple represent the dualistic centripetal and centrifugal forces that converge at the vortex or center of the apple. Looking at the apple from above also resembles the Monad.

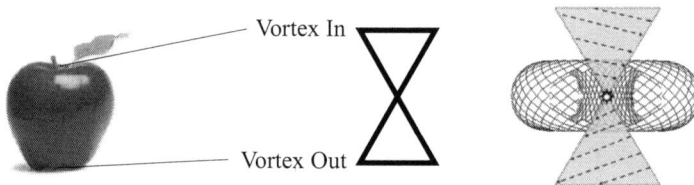

Vortex In

Vortex Out

The geometric torus form is something that we explored in the last volume with the numerical equivalent of the torus equaling the all-powerful 26. The torus is self-referential, self-regenrating and multi-dimensional. It is a perfect blueprint for universal architecture. Could it be that Newton's allegorical story of the apple was not just a reference to the laws of gravity but also to this fundamental, universal shape?

New York City is known as *The Big Apple*. Both *Big* and *Apple* sum to 14, which are representative of your two hands.

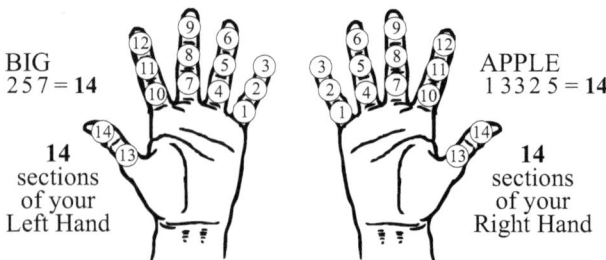

BIG
2 5 7 = **14**

APPLE
1 3 3 2 5 = **14**

14
sections
of your
Left Hand

14
sections
of your
Right Hand

New York City is one the most bustling cities on the globe today. Known as the modern day Rome, New York is a hot spot of commerce, art and fierce individualism. It is unclear as to where the phrase "The Big Apple" originated, but no matter its origin, New York's nickname remains today. *The Big Apple* sums to **46**, which is the identical sum of *Garden of Eden*. In the last volume, we came to find this **46** hiding in the chromosomes of human genetics. There are several very interesting words and phrases that sum to **46**:

THE BIG APPLE
7 6 5 2 5 7 1 3 3 2 5 = **46**

GARDEN OF EDEN
7 1 5 4 5 1 2 6 5 4 5 1 = **46**

KING ARTHUR
3 5 1 7 1 5 7 6 6 5 = **46**

SEED OF LIFE
6 5 5 4 2 6 2 5 6 5 = **46**

THE HOLY BIBLE
7 6 5 6 2 2 2 2 5 2 2 5 = **46**

CANCER / CAPRICORN
3 1 1 3 5 5 3 1 3 5 5 3 2 5 1 = **46**

EQUILIBRIUM
5 4 6 5 2 5 2 5 5 6 1 = **46**

PRIME MERIDIAN
3 5 5 1 5 1 5 5 5 4 5 1 1 = **46**

RIGHT ANGLE
5 5 7 6 7 1 1 7 2 5 = **46**

A person who resides in a city is called a cosmopolitan. *Cosmo* speaks of our universe and politan means "city", therefore, a cosmopolitan is literally defined as a "citizen of the cosmos." New York is a perfect symbol of our universe, an island to itself, deeply inter-connected and only divided through individuality. Busy as a nest of bees and yet, at its heart, merely *one big apple.*

Interestingly, the numerical breakdown of the address of *New York, New York* encodes the Tetragrammaton. New York sums to 22 and there are 7 letters in New York. 22/7 = 3.142. Two of these New York's would come together to give us the Tetragrammaton, or Pi begotten by 7 and Pi begotten by 7.

NEW YORK
1 5 4 2 2 5 3 = **22** / **7** Letters = π

NEW YORK
1 5 4 2 2 5 3 = **22** / **7** Letters = π

New York, New York, as American as *apple pi.*

If we use the mathematical principles of the cross (X, +), we can find several interesting numbers hiding within our *big apple*.

APPLE
1 3 3 2 5

1 x 3 x 3 x 2 x 5 = **90**
1 + 3 + 3 + 2 + 5 = **14** } **90** + **14** = **104**

The **90** degrees, or right angle, of the multiplication of *Apple* and the 14 sections of the hand that holds our apple (found in the addition of apple) come together to give us the swirling circus of stars above our heads known as the *Precession of the Equinoxes.*

PRECESSION OF THE EQUINOXES
3 5 5 3 5 6 6 6 5 2 1 2 6 7 6 5 5 4 6 5 1 2 3 5 6 = **104**

We know from the last volume that precession is the 25,920 year span of time that the sun courses through in its journey through the 12 constellations of the zodiac. We can also find this **104** of our *precession of the equinoxes* in two very interesting places; the Sarsen Circle at Stonehenge measures roughly **104** feet and the two bottom angles of the Great Pyramid of Giza, when rounded up to whole numbers equal 52 and 52 x 2 = **104**. **104** + **76** (or *squaring the circle*) gives us the 180 degrees of our numerical breakdown of the base ten system (*zero - nine* or *one - ten*).

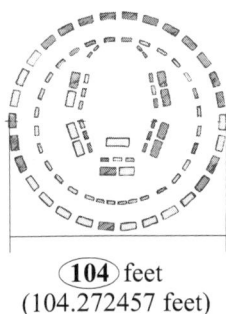

SQUARING THE CIRCLE
6 4 6 1 5 5 1 7 7 6 5 3 5 5 3 2 5 = **76**

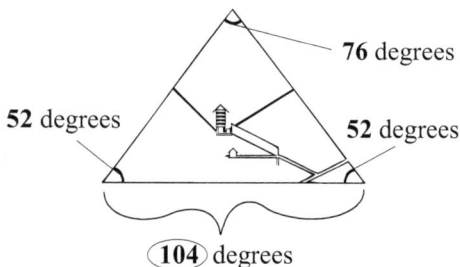

76 degrees

52 degrees

52 degrees

104 feet
(104.272457 feet)

104 degrees

The multiplication of our apple equals 90 and the addition 14. The difference between 90 and 14 is **76**, or *squaring the circle*. Could an apple be used to explain gravity, represent the fundamental form of our universe as well as encode squaring the circle and the precession of the equinoxes? What kind of magic tricks is the universe playing on us? If the fruits of such wisdom are within an apple, it can be no wonder that we took that first fateful bite.

The leaf on an apple is most revealing. Leaves are geometric expressions withholding a bevy of cosmic principles. The first we can easily
derive from the leaf is the unity of opposites, or the symmetrical, mirrored
duality seen between the main vein. It is shaped like the golden womb of
the Vesica Piscis and its veins reflective of the fractal nature of creation.

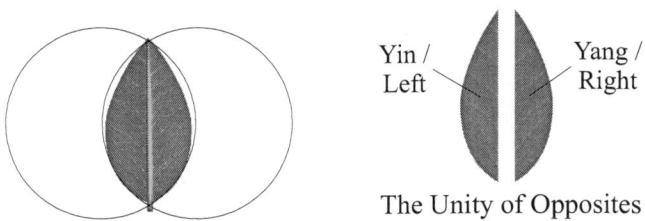

Yin / Left

Yang / Right

The Unity of Opposites

A fractal is a simple mathematical sequence, or set, that can quickly
multiply simple geometric figures into symmetrical, beautiful and lifelike
forms. The basic premise behind this mathematics is that the whole is
within the part and the part is within the whole. This stated philosophically
leads us to our classic Hermetic phrase of "As above, so below". This idea
can also be understood through the hologram. A hologram is a three-
dimensional image formed by the interference of light. Human beings
operate in three dimensions as beings of light (or *hue*-men) so it would
only make sense that we would be holographic in nature. The term
hologram comes to us from the Greek words *holos* (whole) and *gramma*
(message) or the *whole message*. This whole message within the hologram
points to two things that are fractal reflections of each other: the *center* of
our galaxy, (or the *black hole*) which the tail of the constellation *Scorpio*
points to and your *center*. The *torus* making up the dualistic, or *odd/even*,
aspect of the *mother*ly *matter* of our Big Apple has within it the great word,
gramma, or *hologram* of God. We know the symbol of the *LordGod* to be
the Tetragrammaton which is found hiding within the **26** letters of the
English Alphabet.

HOLOGRAM
6 2 2 2 7 5 1 1 = **26**

SCORPIO
6 3 2 5 3 5 2 = **26**

CENTER
3 5 1 7 5 5 = **26**

TORUS
7 2 5 6 6 = **26**

MOTHER
1 2 7 6 5 5 = **26**

MATTER
1 1 7 7 5 5 = **26**

BLACK HOLE
2 2 1 3 3 6 2 2 5 = **26**

ODD / EVEN
2 4 4   5 5 5 1 = **26**

LORDGOD
2 2 5 4 7 2 4 = **26**

ﬡ + ﬥ + ﬡ + ﬢ =(**26**)

He (5) Vov (6) He (5) Yod (10)

A B C D E F G H I J K L M
N O P Q R S T U V W X Y Z

The **26** Letters of the English Alphabet

59 & THE OLYMPICS

The Olympic Games, the world's foremost athletic competition, was inspired by the ancient Olympic Games held in Olympia, Greece from the 8th century BC to the 4th century AD. Olympic means "four years." Every four years we have to add a day to our calendar to account for the roughly 6 hours we gain every year due to our solar year being 365.24 days (.24 is just under 6 hours). The Greeks, like so many advanced cultures of the past, were avid sky watchers and keepers of time. The Greeks followed the *precession of the equinoxes* and believed the Great Year, as they called it, went through four different seasons on its 25,920 year spin. These ages were called the Gold, Silver, Bronze and Iron ages. We know from Volume 1 that these four ages added to 72, which is the number of years it takes the stars to move one degree in precession. In the modern Olympic Games, the top three winning athletes are awarded the *Gold, Silver* and *Bronze* medals. Iron has been dropped from the metals and this makes for a very interesting numerical correlation.

GOLD   SILVER   BRONZE
7 2 2 4   6 5 2 5 5 5   2 5 2 1 1 5 = **59**

By dropping the *Iron* from our great year, this makes the sum of the three metals available to the athletes to be **59**. We know the power of this 59 for not only are there 59 beads in a Christian rosary, but all of the following words and phrases sum to **59** as well.

Jesus Christ, The Holy Name of God, In God We Trust,
English Alphabet, Alchemical Wedding, Alchemical Marriage
Knights Templar, Reborn Christian

The **59** beads of a
traditional Christian Rosary

Are the three medals rewarded to the athletes a symbolic, cryptic reference to the Holy Trinity and Jesus Christ? Classical Greek society flourished in the 4th and 5th centuries BC, long before Jesus Christ ever showed his face. The Greeks celebrated a figure they knew as the *Christos* which shared the same meaning of Christ, that being the annointed, Christened, or enlightened one. Jesus Christ, or **59**, is currently the most well known of these enlightened ones.

47

The Olympic symbol is one of the most easily recognized symbols in the world. Upon its initial presentation, the designer Pierre de Coubertin said of its design: "the six colours (including the flag's white background) thus combined reproduce the colours of all the nations, with no exception."

To include the colors of all nations, let's break down the numerical equivalents of the six colors of the flag, the *white* flag, and the 5 rings being *blue, yellow, black, green* and *red.*

WHITE	BLUE	YELLOW	
4 6 5 7 5 = **27**	2 2 6 5 = **15**	2 5 2 2 2 4 = **17**	27 + 15 + 17 +
BLACK	GREEN	RED	11 + 23 + 14 = **107**
2 2 1 3 3 = **11**	7 5 5 5 1 = **23**	5 5 4 = **14**	

An interesting correlation can be made with the number **107**, for *The United States of America* sums to **107** as well.

THE UNITED STATES OF AMERICA
7 6 5 6 1 5 7 5 4 6 7 1 7 5 6 2 6 1 1 5 5 5 3 1 = **107**

Not only is **107** the 28th prime number (its importance recognized by the 28 phalanges of your hands), but it is also coming up one short from our Holy 108. It is very apparent that the United States was formed long before the logo for the Olympics was created so making this correlation seems rather strange. This **107** is only mentioned here for it will come in handy later in our chapters on Chess and the 12 Disciples of the Zodiac.

The sentiment expressed at the Olympic Games is one of unity. The people of the world come together to compete in the same stadium, toe to toe regardless of race, ethnicity, or country. We come together every four years as equals to reinstate our unity under the heavens above and to commemorate another four years around the Sun. The ancient Greeks, when creating the Olympic Games were reminding the competitors and spectators of the world of two irrefutable facts: The cycle of the sun is the cycle we must follow in order to find the best within us, and no matter how we are divided within this world, we are all equal, for we are *all one.*

THE TETRACTYS

The Tetractys has been the one mathematical symbol that has been consistently used by Pythagoreans, Neo-platonists, Hermeticists, Free-masons and Alchemists alike. This simple pyramid constructed using the numbers 1, 2, 3, and 4 has found a special place in the hearts of the mystics in the past. What is so special about this 10 point pyramid?

```
      •
    •   •
  •   •   •
•   •   •   •
```

The Tetractys was the cornerstone of the ancient Pythagorean schools, a school dedicated to the study of the seven classical liberal arts: number, geometry, music, cosmology, grammar, rhetoric and logic. The Pythag-oreans believed that the universe was a *harmony of spheres* and that this harmony could be intuited by the study of these subjects. The Tetractys provided the Pythagoreans a foundation upon which the mathematics of the creator, or the Grand Architect, could be understood. The Pythagoreans worshiped this symbol so much they even prayed to it.

"Bless us, divine number, thou who generated gods and men! O holy, holy Tetractys, thou that containest the root and source of the eternally flowing creation! For the divine number begins with the profound, pure unity until it comes to the holy four; then it begets the mother of all, the all-comprising, all-bounding, the first-born, the never-swerving, the never-tiring holy ten, the keyholder of all." ~ The Mystic Tetrad

"By that pure, holy, four lettered name on high, nature's eternal fountain and supply, the parent of all souls that living be, by him, with faith find oath, I swear to thee." ~ The Pythagorean Oath

Not much is known about Pythagoras and his followers because the initiates inducted into the Pythagorean schools supposedly swore an oath never to write anything down. Some of the treasures taught at this school have been kept alive though, including the all-too familiar Pythagorean Formula and the much less known Tetractys. Much like the Great Pyramids of Giza, the Tetractys was a key to unlocking an understanding of the Grand Architects archetypal creation. It allowed one a glimpse at the mathemagical inner workings of the universe. It was a pyramid that led one right into the gates of heaven itself.

We are going to take a look at the power of this symbol and the myriad magical things it has to offer within its awesome display of simplicity.

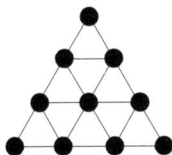

The first four numbers symbolize the harmony of the spheres and the Cosmos as (1) Unity, (2) Dyad, (3) Harmony, (4) Cosmos. The four rows add up to ten, which is the unity of a higher order, or the Decad, represented by the 10 fingers of your two hands. The Tetractys also symbolizes the four elements - Fire, Air, Water, and Earth, as well as giving us the organization of space:

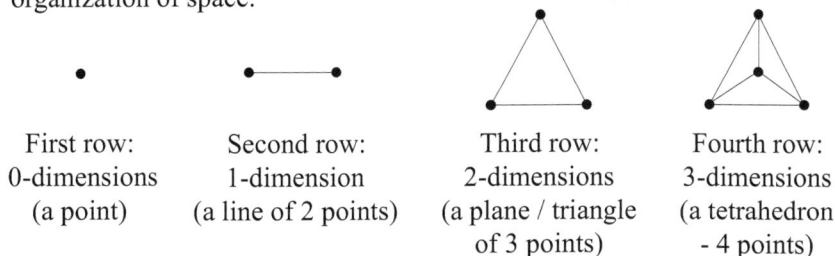

First row:	Second row:	Third row:	Fourth row:
0-dimensions	1-dimension	2-dimensions	3-dimensions
(a point)	(a line of 2 points)	(a plane / triangle of 3 points)	(a tetrahedron - 4 points)

The Greek philosopher Plato assigned numbers to each point on the Tetractys which allows us to peer deep into what it has to reveal.

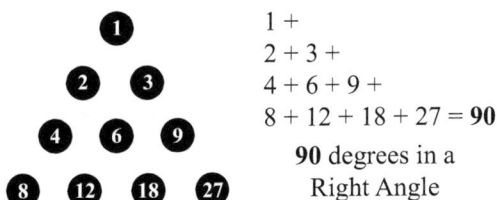

$$1 +$$
$$2 + 3 +$$
$$4 + 6 + 9 +$$
$$8 + 12 + 18 + 27 = 90$$

90 degrees in a Right Angle

The numbers assigned to each point are 1, 2, 3, 4, 6, 9, 8, 12, 18, and 27. Added together, these 10 numbers sum to **90**, or the degrees in a right angle. We can see that there is a doubling pattern and a tripling pattern that delineate the progression of the numbers as they unfold from the capstone of 1. On the left, 1 doubles to become 2 and doubles again to become 4 and doubles again to become 8. On the right, 1 triples to become 3 to triple again to become 9 and triples again to become 27. This doubling and tripling pattern commences down the Tetractys as shown on the illustration on the next page.

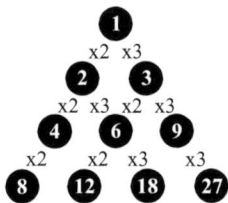

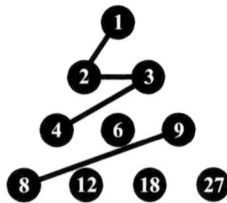

Paging back to our chapter "The Whole Nine Yards," we utilized this multiplication of x2 and x3 on our perfect 3, 4, 5 Pythagorean triangle to find the measurements for two and three English feet. Here again, we find these two principles at work in the holy Tetractys. 2 and 3 according to the Tetractys are *duality* and *harmony,* so we must therefore assume that the Grand Architect is using both *duality* and *harmony* when constructing our universe. The Tetractys even provides us with musical ratios to help us understand that harmony (2:1 - octave, 3:2 - fifth, 4:3 - fourth, 9:8 - whole tone).

We can use decimal parity on the Tetractys and find a whole other set of numbers.

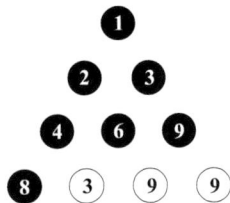

Decimal Parity
Equivalent
1 +
2 + 3 +
4 + 6 + 9 +
8 + 3 + 9 + 9 = **54**

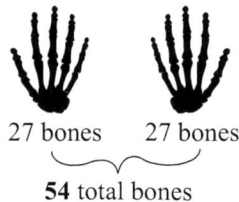

27 bones   27 bones

54 total bones

Notice that using decimal parity, only three numbers had to be converted; 12, 18, and 27 becoming **3, 9,** and **9**. (1 + 2 = **3**, 1 + 8 = **9** and 2 + 7 = **9**). Our decimal parity equivalent Tetractys now sums to **54**. This **54** is a reference to your two hands for each hand has 27 bones, combined to equal **54**. Using the our cipher, the alchemical phrase *Solve Et Coagula,* meaning to "dissolve and coagulate," and the United States phrase *E Pluribus Unum* both sum to **54**. The original Tetractys summed to **90**. **54** added to **90** equals 144, which is 12 English feet. We also recognized in the last volume that not only is 144 the only square Fibonacci number but also the central pillar of our Holy 108 Menorah (see p. 17 of Vol 1). 144 is also a number heavily referenced in scripture (see Revelation 14:1 and 7:4). **90** x **54** equals **4,860**. The interior angles of the Tetractys triangle equal **180**. This added to 4,860 yields the radius of both the Earth and the Moon (**4,860** + **180** = **5,040** miles), the number we find when we *square the circle* of the Earth.

This is just a few different ways that the Tetractys encodes key numbers that help us understand the mathematics of our universe. But it does not end here. The Tetractys has many more tricks up its sleeve.

If we take our original Tetractys and, this time, instead of reducing down our three numbers, 12, 18, and 27, let us instead mirrors those numbers (12 becomes 21, 18 becomes 81, and 27 becomes 72) to find us yet again another treasure buried neath the wisdom of the Tetractys. These 10 numbers now add up to 207.

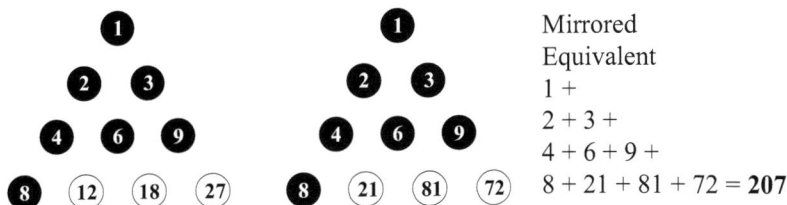

Mirrored
Equivalent
1 +
2 + 3 +
4 + 6 + 9 +
8 + 21 + 81 + 72 = **207**

By sectioning off the 1, or capstone of our pyramid, or by *coming up one extra* we can once again find the number **206** as seen in the eight days of the week (*Sunday - Sunday*) but more importantly, in the number of bones that make up the human skeleton.

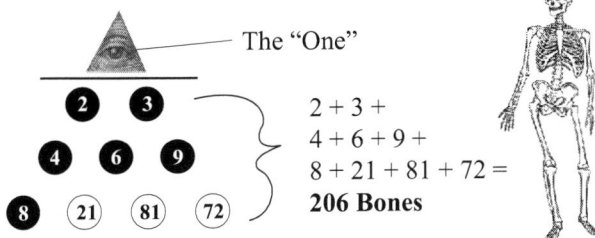

The "One"

2 + 3 +
4 + 6 + 9 +
8 + 21 + 81 + 72 =
206 Bones

By elevating the All-Seeing Eye of God, this also creates the symbols for the four alchemical elements: Air, Earth, Fire, and Water.

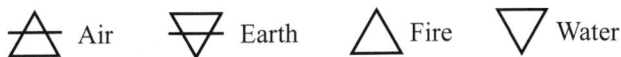

 Air   Earth   Fire   Water

We can even find Pi in the alchemy of the Tetractys. Using the decimal parity reduced Tetractys and adding up the first two rows traveling left, we can find the *Lead* and *Gold* of the alchemical process. The first row sums to 15, or the Gold ($1 + 2 + 4 + 8 = 15$) and the next sums to 12, or the Lead ($3 + 6 + 3 = 12$). The two numbers between 12 and 15, 13 and 14, can be mirrored and combined, as we have done time and time again, to form our mighty, holy Pi (Illustration on opposite page).

$$1 + 2 + 4 + 8 = 15$$

GOLD
$7\ 2\ 2\ 4 = 15$

$$3 + 6 + 3 = 12$$

LEAD
$2\ 5\ 1\ 4 = 12$

LEAD   GOLD

⑫ 13 31 & 14 41 ⑮

π 3.141

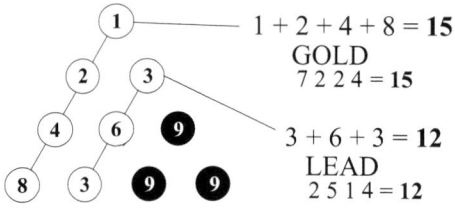

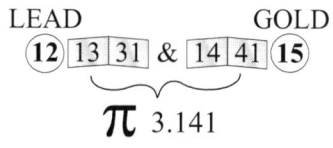

Not only does the Tetractys encode Pi, but it also gives us our 25,920 year precessional cycle. We learned in the first volume that it takes the stars 72 years to move one degree, making a complete cycle in 25,920 years (72 x 360 = 25,920). Looking again at our decimal parity reduced Tetractys, we can separate the first three numbers, 1, 2 and 3, from the remaining 7. By multiplying the bottom rows across and then adding together their sums, we find the number **2,160**. Not only is this 2,160 the diameter of the moon in miles, but it is also exactly 1 age or house of the 12 ages of the Zodiac (12 x 2,160 = 25,920). The numbers 1, 2, and 3 have the very interesting property of sharing the same sum whether added or multiplied (1 + 2 + 3 = **6** and 1 x 2 x 3 = **6**). Adding these two 6s together reveals to us the12 ages of the zodiac.

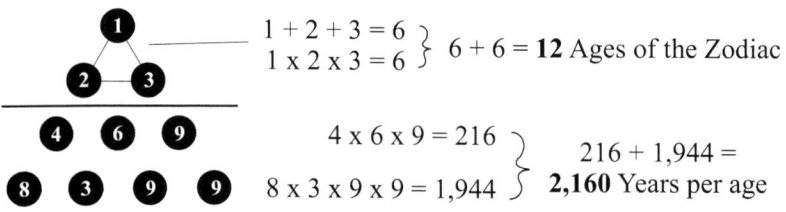

$$1 + 2 + 3 = 6$$
$$1 \times 2 \times 3 = 6$$ $\Big\}$ 6 + 6 = **12** Ages of the Zodiac

$$4 \times 6 \times 9 = 216$$
$$8 \times 3 \times 9 \times 9 = 1,944$$ $\Big\}$ 216 + 1,944 = **2,160** Years per age

Precession of the Equinoxes
(72 year, 1 degree shift x 360) = **25,920** = (12 ages x 2,160 years each)

The four letters of the Tetragrammaton can be used on the Tetractys as well, encoding the 72 year, one degree shift of the precession of the equinoxes as shown below.

ה ו ה י

He   Vov   He   Yod
(5)   (6)   (5)   (10)

10
5 + 10
6 + 5 + 10
5 + 6 + 5 + 10 $\Bigg\}$ 72

In the last volume we touched on the Vortex-Based Mathematics of Marko Rodin, a mathematics that relies heavily on decimal parity. Shown again below is the Vedic "number dial" expressing VBM's infinite circuit. This circuit creates an infinity sign or a pair of "angels wings" in 6 moves using the numbers 1, 2, 4, 8, 7, and 5, with the **3, 6,** and **9** *always separate from the rest.* No matter if we halve or if double within this circuit, we will always and forever end up back at the "One".

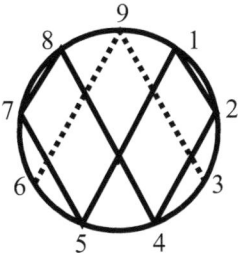

DOUBLING (X2)	HALVING (/2)
1	**1**
1 x 2 = **2**	1/2 = **.5**
2 x 2 = **4**	.5/2 = .25 (2 + 5) = **7**
4 x 2 = **8**	.25/2 = .125 (1 + 2 + 5) = **8**
8 x 2 = 16 (1 + 6) = **7**	.125/2 = .0625 = **4**
16 x 2 = 32 (3 + 2) = **5**	.0625/2 = .03125 = **2**
32 x 2 = 64 (6 + 4) = **1**	.03125/2 = 0.015625 = **1**

We saw this mathematics used in the process of cell division in human reproduction, as well as in the fractions of the Egyptian Eye of Horus myth, and here again it shows its face in the Tetractys. The first line traveling left gives us a doubling pattern of 1, 2, 4, and 8, echoing the Hermapolitan Mystery, "I am the one that becomes the two that becomes the 4 that becomes the 8 that becomes 1 again." We can continue out this doubling eventually to find our infinite number 64 that reduces down to *one*.

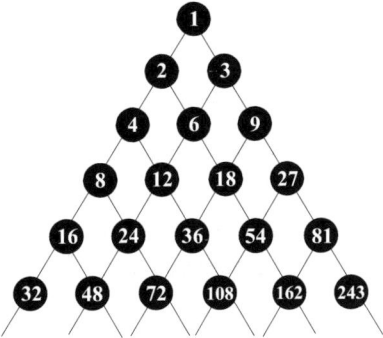

The Tetractys in 6 levels
($\swarrow$ = x2, $\searrow$ = x3)

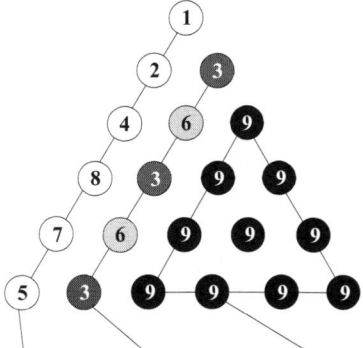

Doubling   Alternating   Prominent
of VBM   **3 & 6**   **9**

Carrying out the multiplication of the Tetractys and breaking it down to its decimal parity equivalent also shows us the prominence of the 9, the alternation of 3 and 6 as well as the doubling pattern of Vortex-Based Math.

We can also find the infinity symbol within the Tetractys as well. Placing our Ennead, or 1 - 9 around the points in the Tetractys and making the zero the central point, we can connect the numbers 1, 2, 4, 8, 7, 5, and 1 to give us a pair of *angels wings*. Also notice that this symbol forms two letters within the Tetractys, **M** and **W**, reflective of the **M**otherly **W**aters of the "eternally flowing creation."

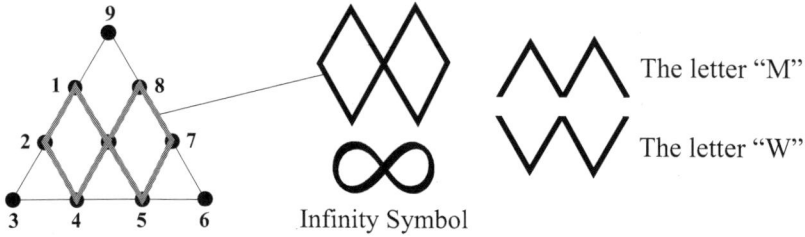

The letter "M"

The letter "W"

Infinity Symbol

Outside the Louvre Museum in Paris sits a glass pyramid designed by the architect I. M. Pei. This name, whether a pseudonym or not, is most interesting since Pe is the Hebrew name for Pi. The architects name sounds more like a proclamation of his knowledge on Pi then anything else: "I Am Pi!" If we highlight the braces in this pyramid, we see that it forms the infinity symbol as well.

The Tetractys has so much to offer us, not only mathematically, but symbolically as well. Only by using decimal parity, can we understand the myriad levels of information the Tetractys has to offer us. This simple pyramid holds within it the magical workings of our universe. It tells us about the mathematics of God and, in turn, tells us much about ourselves. The precession of the equinoxes, the number of bones in the human body, the relationships of 3, 6, and 9, the doubling circuit of cell division and the dimensions of space itself were hiding beneath the numbers of this simple pyramid. The Tetractys was the cornerstone of the Pythagorean schools because it is a cornerstone of the universe.

THE SOLAR SYSTEM

Musica Universalis or The Harmony of the Spheres is an ancient philosophical concept attributed to Pythagoras regarding the proportions in the movements of celestial bodies within our solar system. Pythagoras believed the planets to be related by the whole-number ratios of pure musical intervals, creating a perfect musical harmony. The Solar System consists of 9 planets: Mercury, Venus, Earth, Mars, Jupiter, Saturn, Neptune, Uranus and Pluto. Pluto, considered a dwarf planet, has been recently removed as a part of the Solar System, but we wish to include it here for the very simple reason that no matter how small Pluto is, or how different its elliptical path is, it still nonetheless orbits the Sun. The Sun, or the Solar in our system, sits in the center with its 9 planets revolving around it continuously. This system correlates directly with the Ennead, with the Sun being the center point *or zero*, and the Ennead of 1 through 9 being the planets dancing around their central source. The sun is by far the largest body in the solar system, its diameter being **864**,000 miles. We found this number within the numerical breakdown of the Sun of God, or Jesus Christ with Jesus equaling 27 and Christ equaling 32. 27 x 32 = **864**. Sun worship is seen in every corner of the world, in every single culture, in every single religion. The sun is a giver of life, for its light is the light that lies within us. The giving that the sun does reminds us of the concept of the Holy Spirit or of giving and receiving. The "Spear it" or phallus gives and the vagina or "Wholly" receives. This is indeed why our cosmic source is deemed a *Father* "who art in Heaven" and why we live on *Mother* Earth. The Father and/or Sun's light provides the Earth with energy in its act of giving and the *Mother* of our Earth, who nurtures us as her children, receives this gift with open arms. It is a marriage of cosmic proportions and a love affair that has gifted us the magic of being.

As the Sun courses around the galactic belt or galactic equator, the 9 planets of our Solar System follow it along its way. Through the universal attraction of electromagnetism, the planets chime along with the sun in their own unique orbits. The philosophy of "As above, so below" leads us to the understanding that the body of the solar system must therefore be a reflection of the human body. Like all living things, the solar system is an organized being and is in fact the *Soul of our System*. Every part within it plays a role in making sure that the entire organism functions properly. Every planet has a plan, and every orbit has its place. And they all follow along to the glory of the Sun.

We traditionally have been taught that the planets simply revolve around the Sun, but since the Sun is moving around its central sun, or the black hole of our galaxy, we can get a better picture of what the planets are actually doing on their course through space and time. *The planets are chasing the Sun.*

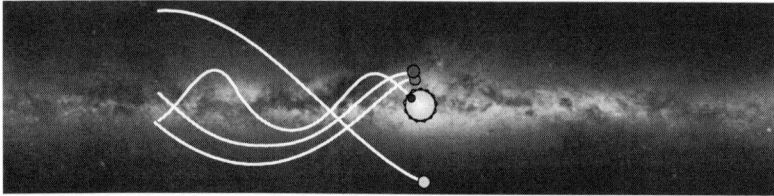

The 9 planets of our solar system are separated by the Asteroid Belt (*or the waist* of the body of the solar system). The division created the rocky planets, Mercury, Venus, Earth and Mars, and the gas giants, Jupiter, Saturn, Uranus, Neptune and Pluto. By assigning the Ennead of 1 - 9 to the planets, making the Sun, once again, zero and utilizing the number dial of Vedic mathematics, we can place our 9 planets around a circle. With the 9, or Pluto at the top, we can draw the diameter down between the 4 and 5 to find the ratio of Pi, which also points us to where the Asteroid Belt, or where the split in our Solar System occurs.

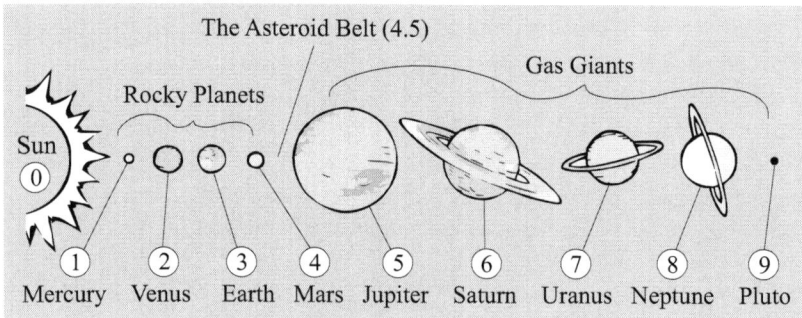

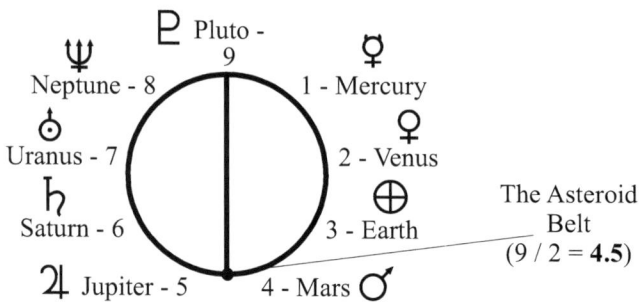

If we correlate this division of our solar system to the division of our seasons here on Earth, with Winter being at the top and summer being at the bottom, splitting our year at the Solstice, we can find a congruence with Cancer and our asteroid belt.

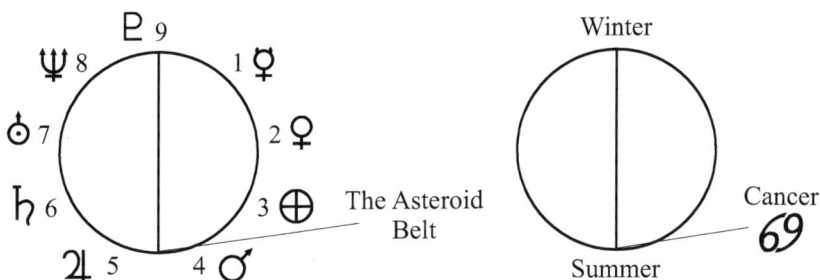

The Asteroid Belt

Solstice means "point at which the sun seems to stand still." During the first days of summer, the sun is at its highest point and stands still in the zodiacal sign of Cancer. We saw in the last volume that the symbol for Cancer, a 6 and 9 nestled with each other, or **69**, pointed us to the three modes of astrology (Cardinal, Fixed, Mutable) and the three phases of alchemy (Nigredo, Albedo, Rubedo).

69
Cancer

CARDINAL   FIXED   MUTABLE
3 1 5 45 1 1 2 + 6 5 3 54 + 1 6 71 2 2 5 = **69**

NIGREDO   ALBEDO   RUBEDO
1 5 7 5 5 4 2 + 1 2 2 5 4 2 + 5 6 2 5 4 2 = **69**

And yet again, we find the number **69** right where it should be.

THE ASTEROID BELT
7 6 5   1 6 7 5 5 2 5 4   2 5 2 7 = **69**

The same symbolic and mathematic principles that work on our seasons here on Earth, work on the solar system as well. The ancients understood that the entire universe operated under strict geometric and numeric principles, and that every organized body, albeit a galaxy or a solar system, is a complete body of work in and of itself. The alchemists often noted the 7 visible heavenly bodies in our sky (Sun, Mercury, Venus, Moon, Mars, Jupiter and Saturn). While the universe seems to be using the principles of the Ennead, the human vehicle on the other hand operates its system under the laws of seven. For not only does the endocrine system consist of 7 chakras, wheels, or energy centers within the body, but as we know the very words we speak find their foundation in the law of 7.

Since the solar system is using the Ennead for its foundation, let's divide 360 degrees by 9, making nine 40 degrees segments. Using decimal parity, we can reduce these degrees down to find a new arrangement for the planets of our solar system (Example - $120°$ would be $1 + 2 + 0 = 3$ or Earth).

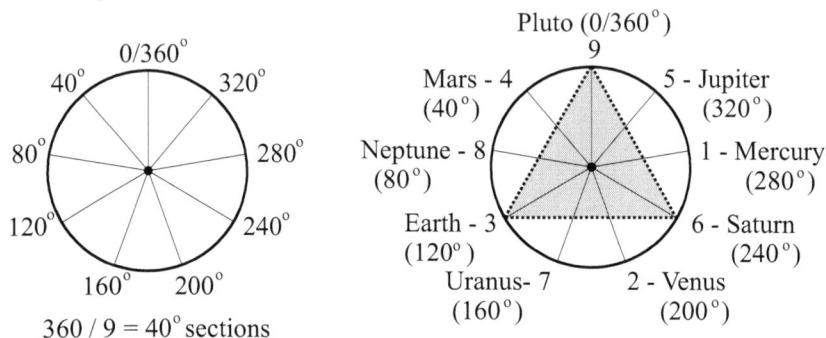

$360 / 9 = 40°$ sections

Pluto $(0/360°)$

Mars - 4 $(40°)$ 5 - Jupiter $(320°)$
Neptune - 8 $(80°)$ 1 - Mercury $(280°)$
Earth - 3 $(120°)$ 6 - Saturn $(240°)$
Uranus - 7 $(160°)$ 2 - Venus $(200°)$

Notice that when the planets are re-situated on the number dial, the **3** and **6** (or Earth and Saturn) alternate and **9** (or Pluto) maintains its place. We can draw an equilateral triangle connecting Pluto, Earth and Saturn to signify their stability. Saturn is known as "the time-keeper" and it is interesting to note that not only is it Earth's counterpart, but it is also the last planet in our system that we can see with the naked eye. By starting at Mercury, or 1, we can weave a line around our number dial by connecting the rest of the planets in order. Remarkably, by doing so, we can create a perfect Enneagram, or nine-sided geometric form.

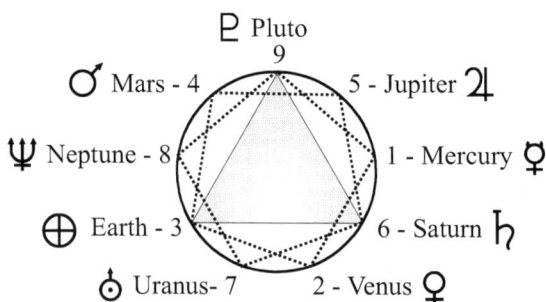

♇ Pluto — 9
♂ Mars - 4   5 - Jupiter ♃
♆ Neptune - 8   1 - Mercury ☿
⊕ Earth - 3   6 - Saturn ♄
♅ Uranus - 7   2 - Venus ♀

Could it be possible that our solar system and the entire universe itself is constructed using such simple, magical tricks of number and geometry? Geometry was sacred to the ancients because it allowed them to see the sort of games God was playing. With the study of geometry came the study of the intelligence behind all of creation.

Using our cipher and applying the numerical equivalents to the Sun and its nine planets gives us a whole new way to see what else the solar system has in store for us.

☉	☿	♀	⊕	♂
SUN	MERCURY	VENUS	EARTH	MARS
6 6 1 = **13**	1 5 5 3 6 5 2 = **27**	5 5 1 6 6 = **23**	5 1 5 7 6 = **24**	1 1 5 6 = **13**

♃	♄	♅	♆	♇
JUPITER	SATURN	URANUS	NEPTUNE	PLUTO
4 6 3 5 7 5 5 = **35**	6 1 7 6 5 1 = **26**	6 5 1 1 6 6 = **25**	1 5 3 7 6 1 5 = **28**	3 2 6 7 2 = **20**

If we add the top row, or the Sun and our rocky planets, Mercury, Venus, Earth and Mars, we yield the number **100** (13 + 27 + 23 + 24 + 13 = **100**). In Volume 1 we discussed the three great crosses that occur in our sky: the Daily Cross (*Sun, Sunrise, Sunset, Horizon*), the Seasonal Cross (*Winter, Spring, Summer, Autumn*) and the Galactic Cross (*Aquarius, Leo, Taurus, Scorpio*), all of which summed to **100**. Percentages are based on the number 100 with 100 perecent meaning "the full amount". How delightful is it that this *full amount* exists everywhere we look?!

The complete 10 heavenly bodies of our solar system sum to **234** (13 + 27 + 23 + 24 + 13 + 35 + 26 + 25 + 28 + 20 = **234**). *360 degrees of a circle* minus the **234** of our solar system = 126 or the 1.26 digits needed for doubling the cube. Using decimal parity, the number **234** reduces down to 9 giving us a direct reference to the structure of the Ennead. If we mirror the number 234, we get 432. The number 432 becomes important for several reasons; There are **4,320** years in two zodiacal ages, the radius of the Sun is **432,000** miles and **432** is roughly the square root of the speed of light in miles per second. 234 mirrored to become 432 also presents us with St. John's number of wisdom for 234 + 432 = **666**.

$$\boxed{234 \mid 432} = \mathbf{666}$$

The numbers **234** and **666** are revealed to us in the very cryptic verse of St. John's Revelation, 13:18, "*Here is wisdom.* Let him that hath understanding count the number of the beast: for it is the number of a man; and his number *is* six hundred threescore *and* six (666)." The number of the verse multiplied together equals **234**. (13 x 18 = **234**). The wisdom St. John speaks of was the wise recognition that his mind or dome was a reflection of the entire solar system. Look around you and welcome yourself home. *This is your kingdome.*

SANTA CLAUS & THE POLES

The story of Santa Claus is the tale of a mythical figure who on Christmas Eve, December 24th, travels across the world in a flying sleigh pulled by 9 reindeer, bringing gifts to good little boys and girls and sometimes lumps of coal to those who were naughty. The story is derived from a Dutch figure called Sinterklaas, which in turn was probably derived from an ancient gift giver named Saint Nicholas. Santa lives in the cold North Pole, where Mrs. Claus and Santa's team of elves prepare all year long for this one joyous day. Being that the origins of this story are rather sketchy, many researchers over the years have tried to piece together what all the elements surrounding Santa mean: flying reindeer, a toy factory full of elves in the North Pole, rewarding kids with gifts and punishing them with coal, and the biggest question of all, why does all this occur on Christmas Eve?

We know from Volume 1 that the days between the Winter Solstice, or December 21st and the three days till Christmas, or December 25th are special days in our solar year. It is this 5 day span that the Sun stops moving South on the horizon, rests for three days only to move one degree North on Christmas, or the day when the *Mass of the Christ* is lifted.

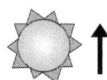

On Dec. 22	Rests for 3 days	Dec 25th
The Sun stops moving South	Dec 22, 23 & 24	Sun moves 1 degree North

Going to *mass* on Christmas Eve is to come together in communion to signify and rejoice the closing and starting of another cycle of life. Christmas day signifies the completion of one year around our great sun or 365.24 days. We've come to know this number from the word *child*, the very people who Santa brings gifts to. It is interesting that Santa chooses to bring lumps of coal to those who were naughty and gifts to those who were nice. This disparity between the two reminds one of the alchemical process with the coal for the naughty akin to the lead and the gifts for the nice akin to the gold. The red and white of Santas dress as well harkens to the Albedo (white) and Rubedo (red) phases of alchemy, the two highest phases in the alchemical process. The only thing absent from Santa's garb is black, or the Nigredo, signified symbolically by the coal given to *unruly* children.

Santa lives in the North Pole. The North and South Poles of Earth are rather inhospitable places. Why would Santa choose this place of all the places on Earth to spend the remaining 364 days of his year? Maybe the answer can be found in number.

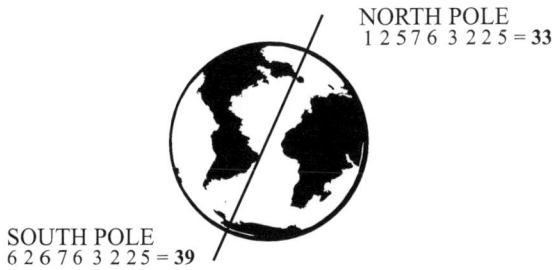

NORTH POLE
1 2 5 7 6 3 2 2 5 = **33**

SOUTH POLE
6 2 6 7 6 3 2 2 5 = **39**

Using our cipher, *South Pole* sums to **39** and *North Pole* sums to **33**. Combined these two numbers gives us the 72 year, one degree shift of the precession of the equinoxes (39 + 33 = 72). We found that many important words and phrases sum to the **39** of our *South Pole:*

Golden Rule, Great Work, Rosalyn Chapel, Freemasonry, Christian

We know the esoteric power of **33** as this number is seen in the story of Christ's missionary and the number of degrees in Freemasonry. Santa living at this 33rd degree is most interesting and speaks volumes on his Sainthood. The North Pole also references the Monad. The poles are where all lines of longitude converge on the Earth. The North and South Pole create the *axis* of the Earth, or the diameter need to find the circumference of the our Earth. Taking a ride in Santa's sleigh and looking at the axis, or diameter of the North Pole from above, we find that Santa's home sits in the center of the Monad.

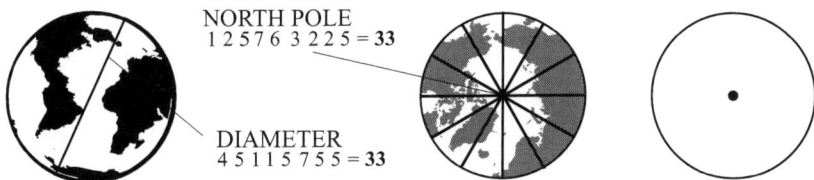

NORTH POLE
1 2 5 7 6 3 2 2 5 = **33**

DIAMETER
4 5 1 1 5 7 5 5 = **33**

The **6** degrees of separation between the *South Pole* or *Christian* of **39** to the *North Pole* or *Diameter* of **33** (39 - 33 = **6**) is also reflective of the process of Kundalini. Kundalini is the ancient Hindu art of raising a serpent energy up one's spine through the 6 chakras, or energy centers within the body, and finally up and out one's 7th, or crown chakra. The practice of Kundalini was the attempt to reach a stage of enlightenment through deep meditation and contemplation (We will revisit these ideas in the section entitled "The 3.5 of Pi"). The number **33**, as we will see, is intimately related to this transcendent state of mind achieved by so many great *saints* of the past.

62

The *Golden Rule,* or the philosophical rule that is shared by so many of the saints and magis of the past, equaling **39** also references the gifts that Santa brings for the children. The naughty and nice deeds done throughout the year are to be weighed at the closing of the cycle. The application of the Golden Rule here is most appropriate for the children who do unto others as they would have done to themselves, will find gifts of gold on Christmas morning. Those who treated others in a malicious or evil way will receive lumps of coal. The Golden Rule comes to us from the concept of the Golden Mean. Mean is defined as a *balancing point* and is the mathematical ratio found in a pentagram, or 5 sided star - the same star that is often found atop our Christmas Trees.

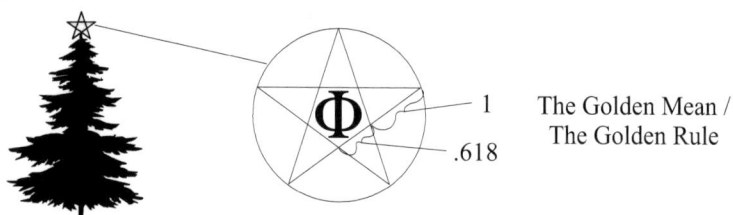

The Golden Mean /
The Golden Rule

The symbol of the tree is one that has been shared throughout the world and is worshiped by the Jewish mystics in the Kabbalistic Tree of Life. The tree is a perfect symbol for all of manifestation and the cycles of time itself. The tree branches out and yet all of its branches unify at the trunk, recognition of the individuality of the personal consciousness and the unification of the collective consciousness of mankind. The entire form of the tree is encased within a single seed, and this seed is reflective of the sacred geometrical Seed of Life and what we have come to know as our primordial egg, or cosmic egg (discussed in Vol 1. in the chapter entitled "The Primordial Egg"). The canopy of the tree provides shelter for man and animal alike, and the tree is in and of itself an entire eco-system. The tree loses its leaves in the Autumn, or Fall, akin to the *fall of mankind*, only to be reborn again in the spring. The tree is crafted by the magical ratio of **1.618**, or the Golden Mean, the ratio seen throughout the natural world. Santa "making his list and checking it twice" is referring to the fact that all of nature records the deeds of human beings and stores them in its collective memory. This field of memory was known as the Akashic records by the Theosophists and comes to us from the Sanskrit words meaning "sky," "aether," or "space." The Akashic records are described as containing all knowledge of human experience and the history of the cosmos. The boys and girls of the world throughout the year add to the collective memory and this saint of Santa records their actions.

The mythical character of Santa Claus therefore is the great *measurer* or *ruler* who records the *balance* or Golden Mean of the children throughout the world. And sure enough, the Golden Mean is found within the name of Santa Claus himself.

SANTA CLAUS
6 1 1 7 1   3 2 1 66 = **34**

16   18

Φ **1.618**

Santa sums to **34**. 34 is a Fibonacci number. We know that the Fibonacci Sequence encodes the Golden Mean of **1.618** by taking a number later in the sequence and dividing it by its predecessor. (Example: 144 / 89 = **1.618**). Since the Fibonacci Sequence can only begin when the first two digits are combined (which are 0 and 1 or our *Wholly* and *Spear it*), we can label 0 and 1 as the 1st term (shown below). A beautiful coherence appears when we term the sequence this way. When we do, the 5 and 5th term line up, the 10th term becomes 55, which using decimal parity *reduces both down to one*, between the 1st term and the 5th gives us three of the musical ratios encoded within the Tetractys (2:1, 3:2, 4:3), and the *12th term*, is 144 with the square root of 144 being *12*. The 9th term becomes **34**, or Santa Claus. We will revisit this breakdown of the Fibonacci Sequence later in the chapter entitled "Chess."

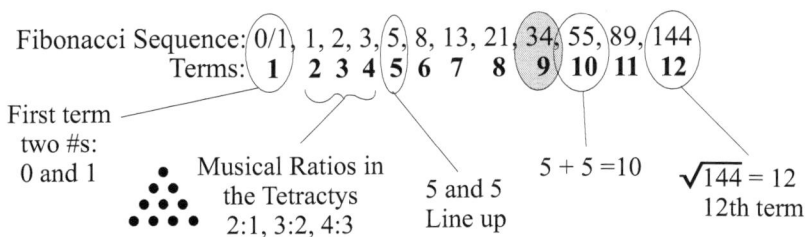

Fibonacci Sequence: 0/1, 1, 2, 3, 5, 8, 13, 21, 34, 55, 89, 144
Terms: **1**   **2 3 4 5 6 7 8 9 10 11 12**

First term
two #s:
0 and 1

Musical Ratios in
the Tetractys
2:1, 3:2, 4:3

5 and 5
Line up

5 + 5 =10

$\sqrt{144}$ = 12
12th term

The 34, or 9th Fibonacci number, reflects the number of reindeer that pulls Santa's sleigh, which in turn is reflective of the Ennead of 1 - 9 with Santa being the zero, or the central sun.

The universe is telling the same story, no matter how many different hands craft it and no matter how many people have their fingers in the pi. The Golden Mean shows its face time and time again, reminding us that if we stay balanced, we won't have to worry about no lumps of coal.

THE 12 DAYS OF CHRISTMAS

In the classic Christmas song, "The Twelve Days of Christmas," a total of 12 different gifts are given to thee by one's loved one. "On the first day of Christmas my true love gave to me, a partridge in a pear tree." The number of each gift that is given is multiplied by the day in which it is given, for instance, on the second day of Christmas, two turtle doves were given, making a total then of 3 gifts; a partridge and two turtle doves. In order to find out how many gifts were given, all we need to do is add up the 12 days of Christmas, or 1 through 12.

$$1 + 2 + 3 + 4 + 5 + 6 + 7 + 8 + 9 + 10 + 11 + 12 = \mathbf{78}$$

Christmas happens only once a year on December 25th, the supposed day of Christ's birth and the day in which the cycle of our solar year starts again. The twelve days of Christmas was known as Christmastide, which started on the 25th and went to the 6th of January. The rebirth of the sun on the 25th of December, *the true meaning of Christmas* has been mostly forgotten but its 12 days still remain glorified in song.

The number 12 has been an extremely important number in religion and mythology. We know of the 12 constellations of the zodiac, the 12 hours of day and 12 of night, the 12 months of the calendar year, the 12 disciples around Jesus, and the 12 sons of Jacob. The square root of 144 is 12. 12 x 360 = 4,320; multiply this by 100 and we yield the radius of the sun in miles. *Why 12?*

Adding the numbers 1 through 12 yields us the number **78.** This number is going to become the foundation for understanding a number of different esoteric and alchemical concepts adored in the past. The original Tarot deck had a total of **78** cards. The Tarot deck, whose origins are unknown, is a system of divination used by occultists and mystics for ages. Currently many people prefer to use the abridged 22 card deck, but classically, **78** cards were used for such magical arts as fortune-telling, astrology and gematria. The Tarot Deck consisted of "The Fool," 21 trump cards (the major arcana) and 56 other cards, divided into 4 suits (the minor arcana). The current 52 card deck widely used in casinos is directly based off the original tarot. The first 5 books of the Old Testament is called the *Torah*, and this is where the name for the Tarot deck is derived (*Torah / Tarot*). In fact, the Old Testament has 39 books and this multiplied by 2 equals **78**.

In our section on the Ennead, we separated the first 9 numbers into 3 levels, or a trinity, reflective of the Christian angelic heirarchy. Walking up the number line to 12 gives us three more numbers to add to our original Ennead: 10, 11, and 12. Added together these three numbers sum to the supremely esoteric **33** (10 + 11 + 12 = **33**). In maintaining our three-fold break-down, we can symbolize the first twelve numbers in our number line by the letter **M**.

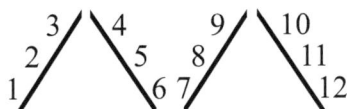

$$\begin{array}{cc} 3\diagup\diagdown 4 & 9\diagup\diagdown 10 \\ 2\diagup\quad 5 \quad 8\diagup\quad 11 \\ 1\diagup\quad\diagdown 6\ 7\diagup\quad\diagdown 12 \end{array}$$

M - Adding 1 through 12 = **78**

In the last volume, we saw that the letter **M** was one of the most important letters in the English Alphabet, for not only did we divide the alphabet at this letter, but the entire alphabet itself can be symbolized with this letter.

$$\begin{array}{cccc} & 7 & & 7 \\ F\,6 \diagup\diagdown 6\,H & & S\,6\diagup\diagdown 6\,U \\ E\,5 \quad 5\,I & & R\,5\quad 5\,V \\ D\,4 \quad 4\,J & & Q\,4\quad 4\,W \\ C\,3 \quad 3\,K & & P\,3\quad 3\,X \\ B\,2 \quad 2\,L & & O\,2\quad 2\,Y \\ A\,1 \quad 1\,M & N\,1 & 1\,Z \end{array}$$

M - 26 Letters of the Alphabet

The letter M is used in astrological symbolism to signify Virgo, the Virgin, a very motherly constellation, as well as Scorpio, the Scorpion, who's tail points to the center of our galaxy.

♏ **Scorpio**   ♍ **Virgo**

The center of our galaxy, our galactic womb or *cosmic mother,* can also be symbolized by the letter **M**, or the first letter in *M*other. The rise and fall of the lines creating the letter **M** has often symbolized water, or fluid movement of time itself. Aquarius, *the water-bearer*, shows the fluidity of the letter **M** in its symbol as well.

♒ **Aquarius**

By separating the numbers 1 through 12 into a trinity, and putting them over the letter **M** this gives us a total of four levels, or lines, to work with. These 4 lines, creating the letter M signify the 4 alchemical elements we know as Earth, Water, Air and Fire. The numerical equivalents of these 4 alchemical elements sum to, not coincidentally, **78**.

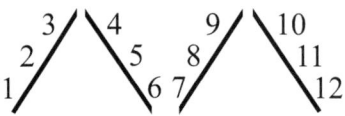

▽	▽	△	△	
EARTH	WATER	AIR	FIRE	
5 1 5 7 6	4 1 7 5 5	1 5 5	6 5 5 5 = **78**	

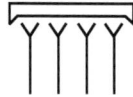

M - Adding
1 through 12 = **78**

The Four Pillars
of Heaven

These 4 lines, levels, or pillars also give us the *four pillars of heaven* known in Egypt as seen in the symbol above. The four pillars create the substantiation of all matter: **Earth** - Solid, **Water** - Liquid, **Air** - Gas and **Fire** - Plasma. They also reference the four fixed signs, or *four horseman of the zodiac,* known by the characters and constellations: Man - Aquarius, Bull - Taurus, Lion - Leo and Eagle - Scorpio, which signify the galactic equator and ecliptic of our solar system. The four alchemical elements are also found on the 12 phalanges of your four fingers. The numerical equivalent of 1.618, the ratio that crafted your hand, encodes the number **78** as well.

Man   Bull   Eagle   Lion

Four Alchemical Elements

Four Fingers: Adding 1 - 12 = **78**

Φ 1.618

ONE POINT SIX ONE EIGHT
2 1 5   3 2 5 1 7   6 5 3   2 1 5   5 5 7 6 7 = **78**

The numbers 1-12 set the foundation for several core principles that are celebrated throughout occultism and esoterica: the 78 cards of the Tarot Deck, the 4 alchemical elements, the 4 pillars of heaven, the 4 fixed points and the 12 ages of the zodiac were all hiding beneath these 12 numbers. But these numbers have even more to offer us.

78 divided by our Holy Trinity gives us the number 26. We know the power of 26 from the Hebraic Tetragrammaton and the myriad other words that sum to 26: *numbers, mother, center, torus, black hole, hologram, odd/even*. By adding the numbers across our **M**, each level going horizontally will sum to 26.

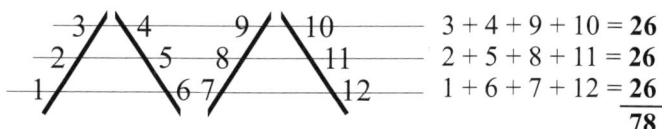

$$3 + 4 + 9 + 10 = 26$$
$$2 + 5 + 8 + 11 = 26$$
$$1 + 6 + 7 + 12 = 26$$
$$78$$

By dividing our base 12 system into 3, this gives us a symbolic alphabet, or *26 letters* for each member of our Holy Trinity, **26** for the Father, **26** for the Son and **26** for the Holy Spirit.

Decimal parity can be used on our base 12 as well, giving us once again, the Tetragrammaton, but this time, in its English numerical equivalent. By reducing down the three numbers we added to our Ennead, or 10, 11 and 12, to their digital root or decimal parity equivalent, we find that our **M** is now flanked by the numbers 1, 2 and 3 (10 = 1, 11 = 2 and 12 = 3). These 12 numbers added together now sum to **51**, or *Tetragrammaton*, with *tetra* meaning four, symbolized by the 4 pillars or lines creating the letter **M**.

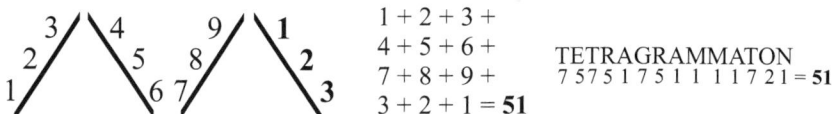

$$1 + 2 + 3 +$$
$$4 + 5 + 6 +$$
$$7 + 8 + 9 +$$
$$3 + 2 + 1 = 51$$

TETRAGRAMMATON
7 5 7 5 1 7 5 1 1 1 1 7 2 1 = **51**

Breaking down the numbers to decimal parity helps us create another symbol as seen below and one we will explore in depth in the next chapter. By highlighting the outside lines of our **M**, or the 1, 2, 3 and 3, 2, 1, we can derive an ancient Egyptian symbol that means to "unite" or "sum up."

Defined as:
to unite,
or sum up

The outside
lines of the **M**
emboldened to signify
the prominence of 1, 2, 3

And we will see that this symbol leads us directly to the 42 principles of the Ma'at, or the Egyptian Book of Law, Order, and Truth. This in turn will bring us full circle back to the holy digits of Pi.

THE EGYPTIAN MA'AT

The Egyptian Ma'at is known as the 42 principles of Law, Order and Truth to which the Egyptians abided. The Ma'at stems from the Old Kingdom with the earliest examples seen as far back as 2,500 BCE. The Goddess Ma'at was she who regulated the stars, seasons, and the actions of both mortals and the deities. The Ma'at were laws set forth by the creator. The feather of Ma'at, or the ostrich feather, is seen in the head dress of the Goddess Ma'at (shown below) and was a symbol often used or adorned by the Gods and Goddess in Egypt to signify their adherence to the creator's laws. Adherence to the Ma'at meant that you preferred harmony to chaos, were undertaking the quest to find your higher, divine purpose and were a constructive member within the community.

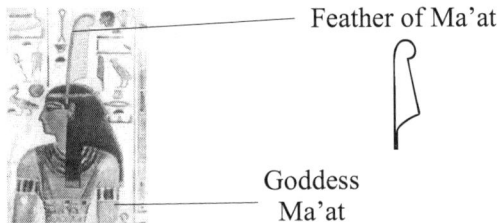

Feather of Ma'at

Goddess
Ma'at

In Volume 1, we saw that the angle of 42 degrees was embedded in the geometry of the rainbow (shown again below). We also learned of the many uses of this number, for **42** is the number with which God creates the Universe in kabbalistic tradition, the number of lines per page in the Gutenburg Bible and the answer to life according to Douglas Adams in his book *The Hitchhiker's Guide to the Galaxy*. The numerical equivalent of *Six* is 14. Therefore, *six six six* would equal **42**.

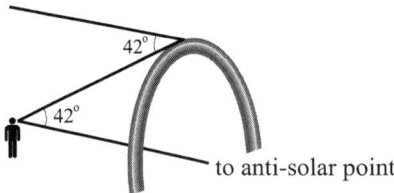

42°

42°

to anti-solar point

SIX   SIX   SIX
653 = **14**   653 = **14**   653 = **14**

42

Walking up the number line we sectioned off the first 12 numbers to find our holy letter **M** and the number of cards in a Tarot Deck. The next three numbers, **13**, **14** and **15** give us those holy digits of Pi. And it is here, right where we find the digits of Pi, we also find the 42 principles of the Egyptian Ma'at for **13 + 14 + 15 = 42**!

69

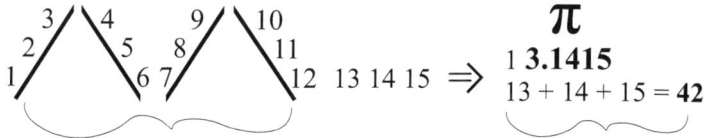

$$\pi$$

1 **3.1415**

13 + 14 + 15 = **42**

78 = 4 Alchemical Elements
Number of cards in a
Tarot Deck

42 Principles of
the Egyptian Ma'at

In Volume 1 we explored these 5 digits of Pi in depth. We saw how they helped create the Garden of Eden as well as help us find the *holy grail* within our own two hands. These three digits become very important, for they hide within them the wholly magic of Pi. Notice that when we create Pi, we are left with 1 digit before the number, with that digit *being one*. If we assign this extra one to the Christ that is within us, we suddenly find a whole new meaning to the phrase *"twelve around one."*

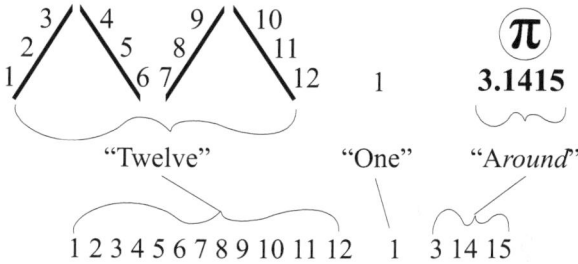

$$\pi$$

3.1415

"Twelve"   "One"   "Around"

1 2 3 4 5 6 7 8 9 10 11 12   1   3 14 15

Using the decimal parity equivalent M as we did in the last chapter, to find the 51 of the English Tetragrammaton, we can now *sum up* or *unite* all parts of our symbol to find this Egyptian symbol of unification.

Defined as:
to unite,
or sum up

The outside
lines of the "M"
emboldened to signify
the prominence of 1, 2, 3

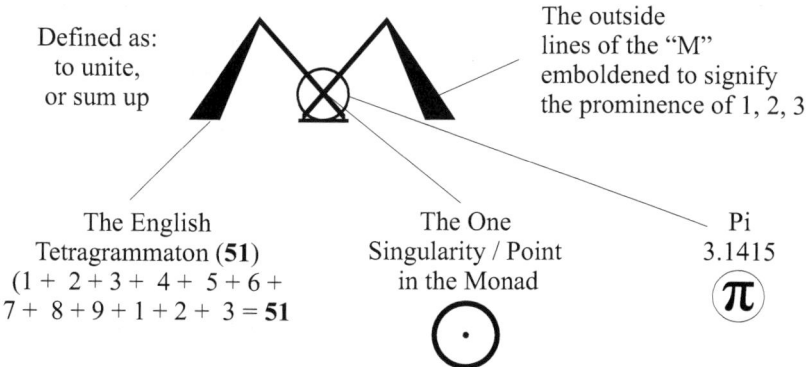

The English
Tetragrammaton (**51**)
(1 + 2 + 3 + 4 + 5 + 6 +
7 + 8 + 9 + 1 + 2 + 3 = **51**

The One
Singularity / Point
in the Monad

Pi
3.1415

$$\pi$$

The holy symbol of **M** is of course the first letter in the word *Ma'at*. It would seem quite obvious that the word *Ma'at* is where we derived the word *math*. *Math* has a numerical equivalent of 15 using our cipher. Many important words share this sum: *human, nous, gold, good, ENKH*. Not only does our Egyptian *Ma'at* end with the number 15, but if we add up each individual number of 13, 14 and 15, *we yield the number 15*. 15 is also nothing more than the mirror of the English Tetragrammaton or **51**.

TETRAGRAMMATON
7 5 7 5 1 7 5 1 1   1 1 7 2 1 = **51**   **15** = 1 1 7 6   MATH

$$1 + 3 + 1 + 4 + 1 + 5 = \boxed{15}$$

With a creative eye, the word *Ma'at* itself encodes the symbols of the 4 alchemical elements, as well as the Christened *one or you*, if we take the Egyptian and Hermetic philosophy of "As above, so below" to heart.

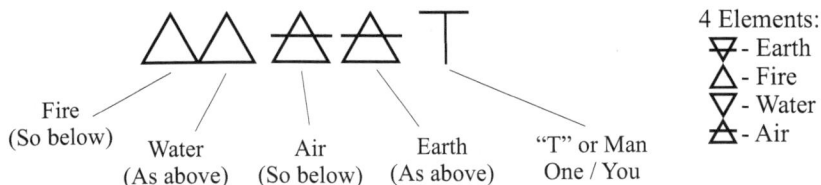

Fire
(So below)   Water   Air   Earth   "T" or Man
         (As above) (So below) (As above)   One / You

4 Elements:
▽ - Earth
△ - Fire
▽ - Water
△ - Air

Seven classical liberal arts were studied in antiquity. This classical curriculum was separated into two different studies: the *Quadrivium* and the *Trivium*. The *Quadrivium* comprises of the four liberal arts of number, geometry, music, and cosmology. *Geometry* is number in space; *music* is number in time; and *cosmology* expresses number in space and time. The *Trivium* was the study of grammar, logic and rhetoric. These seven liberal arts separated into 3 (tri) and 4 (quad) studies are reflective of the sacred geometrical **3** of Heaven and **4** of Earth. Using our cipher, these two classical arts yield some interesting numbers. Not only does the *Quadrivium* gives us the 42 principles of the Ma'at, but combined, the *Trivium* and *Quadrivium* sum to the whole number angle approximate (**76**.3) of the missing capstone on the Great Pyramid of Giza, or **76**.

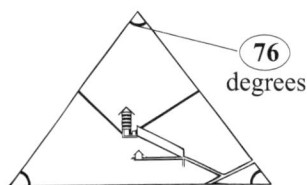

76 degrees

QUADRIVIUM
42 = 4 6 1 4 5 5 5 5 6 1

76

TRIVIUM
34 = 7 5 5 5 5 6 1

What's more? *7 x 6 = 42.*

*Trivium (**34**) + Quadrivium (**42**) =*
Squaring the Circle = 76

71

There can be no doubt that the Egyptian Mystery schools were in fact teaching its initiates about the *mystery of being* and that in order to understand this *mystery*, study of the Trivium and Quadrivium must be undertaken. We can be quite sure that the Platonic and Pythagorean schools were teaching these subjects as well. We should also assume that the mythical Jesus achieved his Christhood by mastering these subjects. The Egyptian Ma'at was a body of knowledge about the underlying laws and physical sciences that governed the cosmos, which existed within the temple, *or body,* of man. Understanding these laws and principles were quintessential to understand thyself. God's work is all around you, but his work does not speak to you in plain English. Only through pattern, number, geometry, symbol and essence can this masterful creation be completely understood. The F*eather of Ma'at* was he who dipped his feather in the ink of knowledge and wrote the story of his life according to the divine laws and principles of the Grand Architect.

Symbols are a language and hold within them clues to understanding the nature of our universe. The occultists and alchemists of the past understood that the geometry and archetypal language within a symbol was as important as any word spoken. Layers of information reside in the simple construction of lines and circles. If we are able to understand and penetrate the creative meanings of our symbols, these layers will unfold and bloom into the flowers of wisdom. Mathematics is the language of God, and if God is hiding within a symbol, the best way to find him is through the sacred power of number.

It seems remarkable that by simply walking up the number line, we can find some of the founding principles of the universe. By *summing up* or *uniting* all of the ideas in a symbol, and understanding what it wishes to say, we can *sum up* all the things it has to offer: the **78** cards of a Tarot Deck, the 12 ages of the Zodiac, the Holy Trinity, the 26 of the Hebraic Tetragrammaton and the 51 of the English Tetragrammaton, the 4 alchemical elements, the Ennead and the 33 degrees of Freemasonry, and last but of course not least, the holy 3.1415 of Pi.

If we've found all this so far, what more lies ahead? Shall we keep walking and find out?

"Climb young lamb up the number ladder, seek your answers and question what you find." - Claudia Pavonis

THE ALCHEMICAL MARRIAGE

In the last few chapters we walked up from 1 - 15 to find the 78 cards of the Tarot deck as well as the 42 principles of the Ma'at. In Volume 1, we saw that the next three numbers in our number line (16, 17, and 18) encode the holy digits of Phi, or **1.618.** The numbers 16 and 18 have their own unique qualities (See "The Holy 108" pg. 19, Vol. 1) and the number 17 nestled between our 16 and 18 has much to offer as we will see in the chapter "153 and the Ark in Scripture."

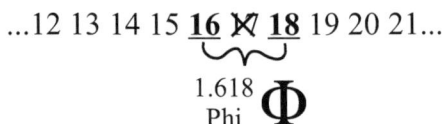

...12 13 14 15 **16** ꓘ **18** 19 20 21...

1.618
Phi **Φ**

We can section off the next 6 numbers in our number line, 16, 17, 18, 19, 20, and 21, to find a symbolic, numeric and geometric metaphor for the ancient alchemical art of merging the opposites within the self, known as the *Alchemical Marriage*.

16 17 18 19 20 **21**

Notice the next six numbers begin with **16** and end with **21**. **16** and **21** added together sum to **37**. We recognized the number 37 from the character of the *unmarried married* or *Virgin Mary*. *Virgin Mary* encodes within her name the marrying of opposites that is metaphorically known as the *Holy Spirit*, or through the homonyms *Wholly* and *Spear it*.

VIRGIN MARY
5 5 5 7 5 1   1 1 5 2 = **37**

We recognized the Greek Monad, the Greek symbol for Phi, as well as the geometry used to find the ratio of Pi, as giving us symbolic represent-ations of the dualistic principles seen throughout the world: giving and receiving or centripetal and centrifugal forces. The *Spear it* of a man's phallus and the *Wholly* of a woman's vagina are recognized in the human being as ultimate expressions of this principled duality - two aspects of one universal motion.

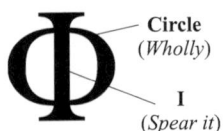

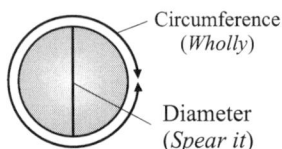

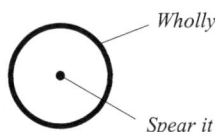

Φ — Circle (*Wholly*) / I (*Spear it*)

Circumference (*Wholly*) / Diameter (*Spear it*)

Wholly / Spear it

Recognizing the duality within the self and *marrying them* to make oneself a fully realized, holistic being was the main goal in the alchemical process. Human beings are reflective of the first thing and the first thing in creation was a *divided, yet unified, androgynous* being - or having the qualities of both male and female. Even children in the womb are considered androgynous until around the 49th day when the sex of the child is finally determined. Though we are born as either male or female, all of us continue to have this initial duality within us. In order to become one with the supreme source, those dualities must unify - mythologized in the *Hermaphroditic* Hermes, or the unified characters of the Hermes and Aphrodites.

Recognizing the symbolism of the *Holy Spirit* gives us two geometric forms to work with, a circle and a line. We can view this circle and line or 0 and 1 as we did in the Garden of Eden in Volume 1, or as the mythological Adam (odd) as 01 and Eve (even) as 10.

O | | O

This circle (*Holy*) and line (*Spirit*) are two of the most basic shapes in existence, yet direct us to one of the most fundamental mathematical principles that exists throughout the world. This line and circle, or zero and one, actually marry each other to begin the Fibonacci Sequence, or the sequence used to find the 1.618 of Phi. The sequence starts out by adding 1 to zero to find the first sum of the Fibonacci sequence to be the all-unifying *One* ($0 + 1 = One$). It is the paradoxical duality of both line and circle coming together to become *one*. The growing spiral complexity of the Fibonacci Sequence stems from these two numbers. We see the same complexity of nature mimicked in technology. The worldwide web, or internet, is the most complex integrated system of networking ever conceived. Videos, pictures, text and graphics are all uploaded and shared by people around the world, and all of this data is processed at near the speed of light. The entire internet, in all of its complexity is based off two numbers, 0 and 1, called a binary code. Binary code is the coding also used in the ancient Chinese divinatory system of the *I Ching*, or *Book of Changes*. This zero and one and their alchemical marriage even work in the world of computing with zero being *on* and one being *off*. Just think, every time you surf the *net* (or *ten* spelled backwards), the Holy Spirit is staring at you out of your computer monitor.

We understand the unity of opposites to be the merging of man and woman. We can numerically find this opposites in the royal terms used throughout the ages; the *King* and the *Queen*.

KING
3 5 1 7 = **16**

QUEEN
4 6 5 5 1 = **21**

King sums to **16** and *Queen* sums to **21**, together equaling **37**. By sectioning off the numbers 16 - 21 in our number line, we can now put the *King* at the beginning and the *Queen* at the end to encapsulate our 6 numbers.

KING
3 5 1 7 =⑯——(**16**)17 18 19 20(**21**)——㉑= QUEEN
4 6 5 5 1

The King and Queen represent the dualistic aspects within the self. In order to complete the alchemical marriage, they would have to unify. The *King*, or *Spear it* would need to find his *Wholly Queen*. We can find these opposites in the world of music. There are two distinctions for notes on a musical scale which are not considered Whole (or what we will consider as *un-unified*) known as *Flat* and *Sharp*. Using geometry as our guide, we can assign the *Flat* to be the circle of the *Wholly Queen* and the *Sharp* to be the line of the *Spear it King*. Notice when we do this, *Sharp* equals 21 and *Flat* equals 16, together summing to once again, **37**. With the *Sharp/King* and *Flat/Queen* we now have two **37**s summing to a total of **74**.

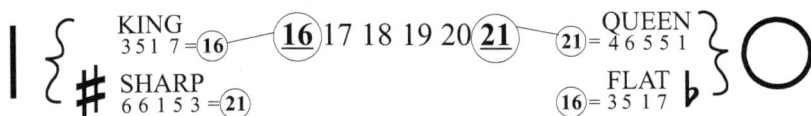

KING
3 5 1 7 =⑯——(**16**)17 18 19 20(**21**)——㉑= QUEEN
4 6 5 5 1

♯ SHARP
6 6 1 5 3 =㉑

⑯= FLAT
3 5 1 7 ♭ ◯

The two alchemical marriages, *King* and *Queen* and *Sharp* and *Flat* summing to **74**, is interesting for two reasons: One, if we add up the four numbers between 16 and 21 they sum to **74** (17 + 18 + 19 + 20 = **74**). Two, **74** is found on the eternal opposites of your two hands.

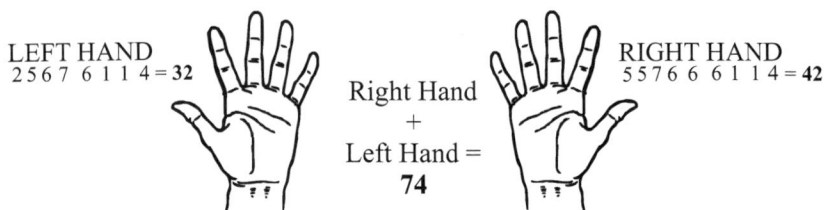

LEFT HAND
2 5 6 7 6 1 1 4 = **32**

Right Hand
+
Left Hand =
74

RIGHT HAND
5 5 7 6 6 6 1 1 4 = **42**

The *King* and *Queen* and the numbers they encapsulate can also be used to help us find the digits found in the numerical equivalent of the word Phi or the **365** days in a solar year. Multiplying the *King*, or 16, by the *Queen,* or 21, equals **336** (16 x 21 = **336**). Adding the individual digits of the four numbers we have left results in the number **29**. The multiplication of the *King* and Queen added to this **29** gives us the **365** days of our solar year as well as the **365** in the letters of Phi.

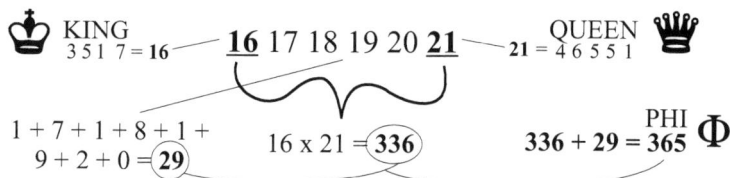

♚ KING
3 5 1 7 = 16 ———— **16** 17 18 19 20 **21** ——— 21 = 4 6 5 5 1 QUEEN ♛

$1 + 7 + 1 + 8 + 1 +$
$9 + 2 + 0 = $ **29**   16 x 21 = **336**   336 + 29 = **365** PHI Φ

We can also find the **336** of our *King* and *Queen* in the numerical equivalent of *The United States of America* which, like the 6 colors of the Olympic Flag, sums to **107**. **107** multiplied by Pi, or 3.14, equals **336**. (107 x 3.141 = 335.98) This is something we will explore in depth in the next chapter and in the chapter "The 12 Disciples of the Zodiac."

Adding up our 6 numbers, 16-21 equals **111** (16 + 17 + 18 + 19 + 20 + 21 = **111**). These three ones harken to the geometry of the first form in existence. These three lines represent the 3-fold, triune principle of the world, the three sides of the triangle coming together as one. This three-fold aspect of God, as we know, is also known as the three Big Os: *Omnipotent, Omniscient* and *Omnipresent.* Together they sum to **111**.

OMNIPOTENT   OMNISCIENT   OMNIPRESENT
2 1 1 5 3 2 7 5 1 7 = 34   2 1 1 5 6 3 5 5 1 7 = 36   2 1 1 5 3 5 5 6 5 1 7 = 41 } **111**

In order to truly understand how God could be everywhere at once, one would have to make himself whole, holy, or at one with the whole of creation. Any division within him was a division from the true nature of this holy/wholly existence. Merging the halves within the self, the spirit with the matter, and the yin with the yang produce a wholeness of self that allows one to be at one with the undifferentiated light of the first thing in creation. Following the Trinity (**111**) allows one access to the first moments of creation, as Genesis will forever remind us.

AND GOD SAID, LET THERE BE LIGHT
1 1 4   7 2 4 6 1 5 4   2 5 7 7 6 5 5 5 2 5 2 5 7 6 7 = **111**

And we should also mention that *Let there be light* equals **76**.

CHESS

The game of chess is a timeless game. Played throughout the world, fans of chess range from the very young to the very old. Though the origins of chess are unknown, it does seem to be based on a similar game called Shantraj from India that is quite possibly thousands of years old.

Chess is a highly mathematical game, though most who play it hardly ever think of numbers when deciding their next move. Chess is composed of 64 squares (32 black and 32 white) with 16 pieces per side (1 King, 1 Queen, 2 Rooks, 2 Knights, 2 Bishops and 8 Pawns). The object is for each player to overtake or *checkmate* the other's King. Each piece has its own qualities and particular movements: the Pawn can only move forward, the Rook side to side, the Bishop diagonal, the Knight leaps up and over, the King may move one square at a time and the Queen may basically do whatever she wishes. Each piece has its own particular starting place on the board. Shown below is where each piece is placed at the start of the game.

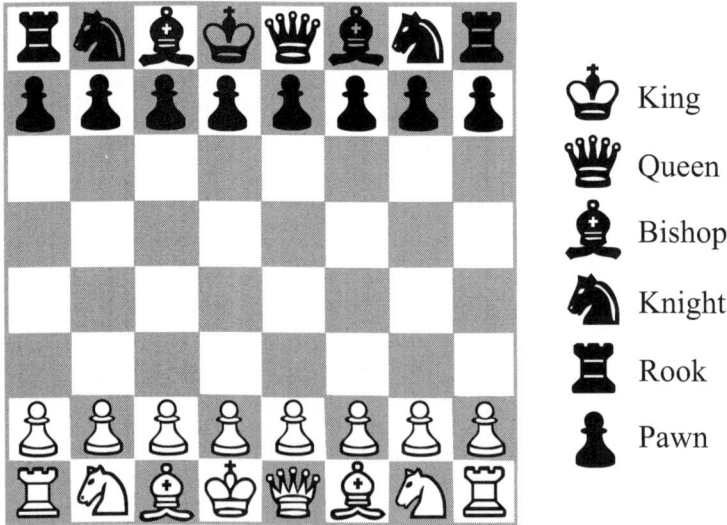

King

Queen

Bishop

Knight

Rook

Pawn

Our look at chess will not concentrate on the game itself or the moves of the players. Instead, by using our cipher, we will discover that hiding within the game of Chess lies not only our holy Pi, but also a lunar, solar and precessional calendar. Before we assign all the numbers to the letters of the pieces, let's first look at the board itself.

The 4-sided chessboard consists of **64** squares. In Volume 1 of this text, we looked at this number **64** in depth. This very important number has been expressed throughout history in multitudinous ways: there are 64 spheres in the 3 dimensional rendition of the sacred geometrical Flower of Life, there are 64 positions in the Kama Sutra, there are 64 hexagrams that compose the ancient divinatory text of the I Ching and the Chinese game, the Tower of Hanoi consists of 64 discs. We attributed the importance of this number to the fact that the genetic instructions for all of life, called DNA (deoxyribonucleic acid), consist of 64 codons. Could it possibly be that the ancient people who crafted the game of chess intimately knew the workings of our DNA? Though we can only speculate, it would seem that the repeated appearance of this number must have a deeper significance, and nothing could be more significant than the number for the instructions of life. The 64 squares on a board are split into two colors making **32** black and **32** white squares. We have also recognized the power of **32** for not only does the second highest degree of Freemasonry climb to **32**, but many other words and phrases find this sum as well:

Present, English, Lucifer, Freemason, Trinity, Axis Mundi,
King Solomon, Christ, Holy Grail, Gematria, Religion

If we add up all the digits from 1 to **32**, this will sum to **528**. Multiply this by 10 and, we find the number of feet in an English mile or **5,280**.

With 16 pieces per player taking up 32 squares, this leaves the initial battlefield of 16 black and 16 white squares. The King himself (as we will see in just a bit) equals 16 as well. Utilizing specific numbers such as 8, 16, 32 and, 64, Chess allows for a near infinite amount of moves to be made within the confines of the closed infinity of the game. 64 is an infinite number, for it is **8** squared (8 x 8 = 64), with the symbol for the number 8 being the classic infinity sign stood upright.

$$\infty \quad 8$$

Chess is **1** game for **2** players, with **4** sides to the board, consisting of **8** squares per side, **16** pieces per player, **32** squares of each color, with a total of **64** squares: **1, 2, 4, 8, 16, 32, 64**. Not coincidentally, we saw these exact same numbers in Marko Rodin's Vortex-Based Math, as well as in the Egyptian Eye of Horus myth (illustrations on following page).

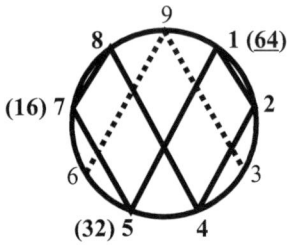

Vortex-Based Math	Eye of Horus	CHESS:

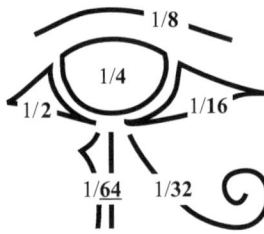

CHESS:
1 game
2 players
4 sides
8 squares per side
16 pieces per player
32 squares of each color
64 squares

The chessboard motif is a motif used across the world. Many floors in Freemasonic halls or temples, as well as in many of their illustrations, are decorated with the chessboard floor and there can be no doubt that this pattern is a direct reference to this ancient game. The simple alteration of black and white squares speaks directly to the unity of opposites within the world and the battle between players, black and white, a representation of the eternal battle between good and evil. The chessboard is yet another expression of yin and yang interlaced or *woven together* in the material world. The game itself represents the journey one takes through the rigors of life, and the rules of the game are akin to the laws of nature as Thomas Henry Huxley so elegantly exclaims:

> The chess-board is the world; the pieces are the phenomena of the universe; the rules of the game are what we call the laws of Nature. The player on the other side is hidden from us. We know that his play is always fair, and patient. But also we know, to our cost, that he never overlooks a mistake, or makes the smallest allowance for ignorance.

There is no law more important to humans than the law of time. Time is the stage upon which all phenomena occur, and understanding the cycles of time was of utmost importance to our ancestors. In Vol. 1 we saw that the 364 day year was encoded in the traditional deck of cards (see Jachin & Boaz, pg. 41) so it should be no surprise to find that a calendar, *or calendars,* are encoded in the game of chess as well. In order to understand how to build these calendars, first we are going to have to assign the numerical equivalents for each piece of chess. The first piece we will assign numbers to is the piece that is seen most on the board or the Pawn. And lo and behold, Pawn gives us those holy digits of Pi, 3.141.

PAWN
3 1 4 1

Below are the numerical equivalents for each game piece:

PAWN	ROOK	KNIGHT	BISHOP	QUEEN	KING
3 1 4 1 = **9**	5 2 2 3 = **12**	3 15 7 6 7 = **29**	2 5 6 6 2 3 = **24**	4 6 5 5 1 = **21**	3 5 1 7 = **16**

These 6 characters create the entire game of chess. In the last chapter we noticed that by walking up our number line, the King and Queen sectioned off 6 numbers, 16, 17, 18, 19, 20, and 21, with the numbers between the King and Queen equaling 74 (7 + 18 + 19 + 20 = 74). All the numbers combined summed to **111**, resonating with Genesis 1:3 as well as the words *Omnipotent, Omniscient* and *Omnipresent*. We see this exact same thing with the 6 players of Chess. Pawn, Rook, Knight and Bishop sum to **74** with the King and Queen added to sum to **111**.

PAWN   ROOK   KNIGHT   BISHOP   QUEEN   KING
3 1 4 1 + 5 2 2 3 + 3 15 7 6 7 + 2 5 6 6 2 3 + 4 6 5 5 1 + 3 5 1 7 = **111**

We can now assign the numbers for each piece to each side of the board. This will help us de-construct the numerology within the game.

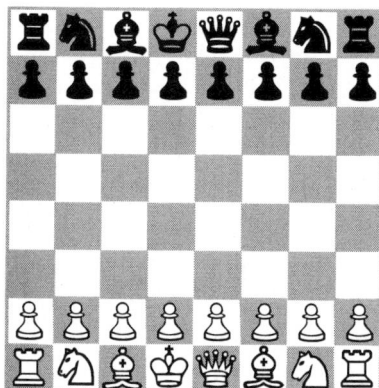

Before we look into constructing the calendars though, let's first concentrate on the verbiage surrounding Chess, or the words: *Chess, Check* and *Checkmate*. In the game of chess, when one's opponent has the other's King cornered or has the ability to capture the King within the next move, the person says "Check!" If one has the other opponent's King cornered and the opponent is unable to make another move, this is called *Checkmate* and means that one has won the game. Let's take a look at the numerical equivalents of these words.

80

CHESS	CHECK	CHECKMATE
3 6 5 6 6 = **26**	3 6 5 3 3 = **20**	3 6 5 3 3 1 1 7 5 = **34**

The first thing that one should notice is that all three words begin with CHE or **365**, which is of course the number of days in a solar year. Chess sums to 26, which we know as an all-powerful number, for it is the number of letters in the English Alphabet as well as the numerical equivalent of the Hebraic Tetragrammaton and our *LordGod*. *Check* sums to 20 which is the number of fingers for both players in the game (10 fingers for white and 10 for black). Adding up all three of the words *Chess*, *Check* and *Checkmate* sums to 80 (26 + 20 + 34). In the Greek gematria Pi had the numerical equivalent of 80, and Pi in our cipher sums to 8 which is nothing more than a division of 10. Also, using decimal parity, 80 reduces down to 8, and the board is based on the number 8.

Understanding the word *checkmate* is a little more difficult and requires us to once again look at the Fibonacci Sequence. Each term in the sequence is labeled as we did in our section on "The 12 Days of Christmas" as shown again below.

Fibonacci Sequence: 0/1, 1, 2, 3, 5, 8, 13, **21**, **34**, 55, 89, **144**
Terms: 1   2 3 4 5 6 7 8 9 10 11 12

Queen   Checkmate!

16 Pawns
(16 x **9** = **144**)

In order for one to win the game, one must *Checkmate* or move off the infinite board of 8, or the *8th Fibonacci number* (or **21**, which is the numerical equivalent of the *Queen*, the second strongest piece on the board next to the *King*) and onto the 9th Fibonacci number, **34** or *Checkmate!* Adding up all the Pawns in our game yields us the number **144** (Pawn = 9, 9 x 16 Pawns = **144**), the *12th number of the Fibonacci sequence.* Adding up only one team of Pawns, or 8 total, sums to **72** (8 x 9 = **72**). We know that the precessional time is counted by the 72 year/1 degree span of time and this row of Pawns is in fact informing us of this measurement of time. In order to calculate our precessional Great Year, we need to multiply our 72 x 360 to find 25,920 years. Since the Pawn itself refers to Pi we know we must be dealing with 360 degrees, so our math becomes apparent. Even the head of the Pawn speaks to us about the power of the circle.

π PAWN
3 1 4 1 = **9**   360 Degrees

When was the last time that you played chess, moved your first pawn forward, and simultaneously thought about the infinite digits of Pi or the great cycles of our zodiac? Not only do the pawns encode the Precession of the Equinoxes, but the multiplication of the numerical equivalent of Chess does as well.

CHESS
36 5 6 6

3 x 6 x 5 x 6 x 6 = 3,240. Since Chess is *a game based in 8*, we may multiply the multiplication of the Chess by our infinite **8** and find our **25,920** years (3,240 x 8 = **25,920**).

CHESS
36 5 6 6 (3 x 6 x 5 x 6 x 6) = 3,240   3,240 x **8** = **25,920**

Since we've looked at *Chess/Check/Checkmate* and the *Pawn*, let's now turn our attention to the most powerful piece on the board, the King. The letters above Jesus Christ when he died were **INRI** and it meant, "Jesus of Nazareth, *King* of the Jews." Both *King* and *INRI* sum to 16, and this is no coincidence.

KING   INRI
3 5 1 7 = **16**   5 1 55 = **16**

The number **16** becomes very important in the game of chess. In order to win the game, one must ultimately capture the **16** pieces of one's opponent, secure the **16** opposite-colored squares on the initial battlefield and topple the *King* who sums to **16** as well. The numerical equivalent of the King becomes the foundation for the rules of the game. The board is an 8 x 8 board with the squares divided into 32 black and 32 white squares. Interestingly enough, the numerical equivalent of *Sixteen* sums to 32 as well.

SIXTEEN
653 755 1 = **32**

As we saw in Volume 1, a square with a length of its side being 4 will have the very peculiar quality of having both its circumference and area be equal (Area: 4 x 4 = **16** and Perimeter: 4 + 4 + 4 + 4 = **16**). Besides 18, this is the only natural number with this property, and this is assuredly the reason why chess, a game based solely around squares, utilizes this number. Sixteen is also the place in our number line where the digits of Pi cease.

11 12 13 14 15 **16**

The Sixteen of the King leads us to her eminence the Queen.

The Queen is the most powerful piece next to the King. Combined, the 16 of King and the 21 of Queen sum to **37**. Using decimal parity and reducing down the numbers for the King, or 16 to **7,** and the Queen, 21 to **3,** this gives us, once again, the numbers 3 and 7. Since we found a Pre-cessional calendar within the numerical equivalents of the words *Pawn* and *Chess*, there should be no doubt that we can find something similar within our two royalty. As we saw in the last section, by multiplying the King and Queen together and then adding the individual digits between 16 and 21, these two numbers will sum to 365, or the 365 days of our solar year as shown again below.

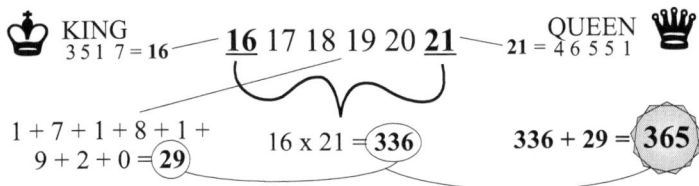

We can also find this 29 needed to complete our solar year in the *Knight*, summing to 29. By multiplying the King and Queen and adding a *Knight,* we yield **365** days. The King and Queen multiplied together sum to **336** (16 x 21 = **336**). We can also find this **336** hiding in *The United States of America*.

THE UNITED STATES OF AMERICA
7 6 5 6 1 5 7 5 4 6 7 1 7 5 6 26 1 1 5 5 5 3 1 = **107**

The United States of America, or **107** x Pi (3.14) = 335.98 (or rounded up to **336**). Understood numerically, the United States in its numerology seems to encode the alchemical marriage of the monarchy of the King and Queen.

Since the Pawn, as well as the King and Queen, seem to be each holding wisdom on the cycles of our heavenly bodies and stars within their numbers and symbolism, let's see what the rest of our battalion has in store for us. We can now remove the King and Queen, as well as the Pawns in the game, and just utilize the pieces we have left. By using the pieces on both sides of the board, we will come to find a perfect lunar calendar exquisitely and artfully encoded in the game (illustrations on next page).

83

| 12 | 29 | 24 | | 24 | 29 | 12 |

| 12 | 29 | 24 | | 24 | 29 | 12 |

ROOK
5 2 2 3 = **12**

KNIGHT
3 1 5 7 6 7 = **29**

BISHOP
2 5 6 6 2 3 = **24**

By focusing only on our *Rook*, *Knight* and *Bishop*, this allows us to use the remaining squares on our board (or where the King and Queen were) to our advantage. The first thing that we should notice is that *Rook* sums to **12** and *Bishop* sums to **24**. These numbers directly reflect the hours of our day, **24** in one day and **12** in a half day. In assuming that the creators of chess intended these numbers to represent the hours of our day, then all we are left with is the **29** of our *Knight*. The word *Knight* is most interesting. Why in the world is Knight spelled with a **K**? There is absolutely no need for this letter to be in the word since the first sound when spoken is an **N** sound. The **K** becomes important in pointing us in the right direction for without this **K**, night would only sum to 26. The numerical equivalent of *Knight*, or **29**, leads us to our *night* skies and the always feminine Moon. A synodic lunar month, or the time period between new and full moons, is a time span of **29**.5 days.

Synodic Lunar Month =
29.5 Days
(29.53 days exactly)

If the **Knight** is indeed pointing to this calendrical time period, then we seem to be missing the half, or **.5** day in our lunar month. Since Chess is only using whole numbers, this half day must be hiding within the other pieces somewhere. By connecting each piece, placed symmetrically on the board, with semi-circles (or the branches of the menorah once again), we can establish a relationship between the hours of the day denoted by the *Rook* and the *Bishop* to the number of days in a lunar month denoted by the *Knight*. Doing this also allows us to utilize the empty squares once occupied by our King and Queen (illustration on next page).

84

$$24 + 24 = (48 \text{ hours})$$
or **2 days**

$$29 + 29 = \textbf{58 days}$$

$$12 + 12 = (24 \text{ hours})$$
or **1 day**

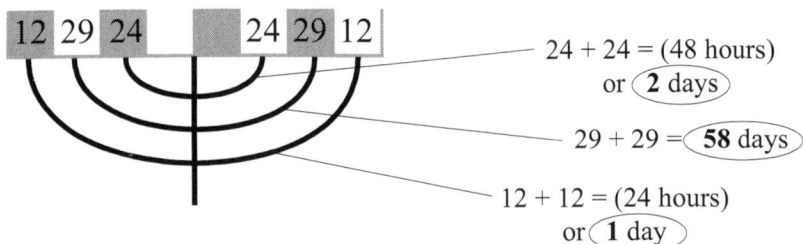

Notice that by converting the 24 hours given to us by our two rooks and combing two whole number lunar months of 29 days, this allows us to make up for the **.5** and **.5** day missing from both our Knights or lunar months. This is shown below for clarification.

Synodic Month =
29.5 Days

Knight (**29**) + Knight (**29**)
.5   .5

.5 + .5 = **1 day**
Rook (12 hrs) + Rook (12 hrs) = **1 day**

By understanding that our Bishops and Rooks are converted from hours to days, this establishes a relationship between the pieces. If **1** day is to **58** days, then **2** days must be double this, or **116** days. We can place this **116** days within the empty squares of the King and Queen, or exactly where the central pillar of our menorah leads us.

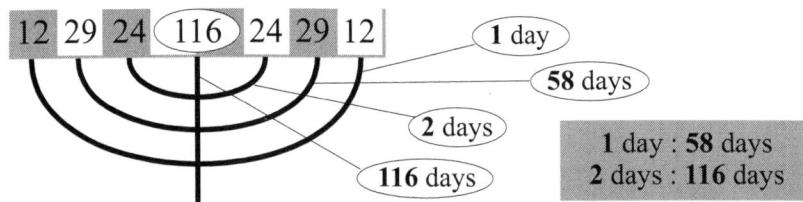

1 day

58 days

2 days

116 days

1 day : 58 days
2 days : 116 days

If we add the total number of days given to us by the 6 pieces, this will sum to **177** (1 + 2 + 58 + 116 = **177**). By converting our *Bishop* and *Rook* to days (and hence decimals for the *Rook*), and we perform this trick on both sides of our board, we can find the number of days in 12 synodic months, or **354** days (117 x 2 = **354** and 12 x 29.5 = **354**).

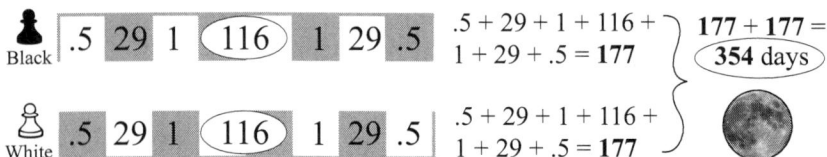

Black   .5 29 1 (116) 1 29 .5

.5 + 29 + 1 + 116 +
1 + 29 + .5 = **177**

177 + 177 =
354 days

White   .5 29 1 (116) 1 29 .5

.5 + 29 + 1 + 116 +
1 + 29 + .5 = **177**

By encoding a lunar, solar and precessional calendar in the game, the creators were clearly notifying us about their obsession with time. Following the cycles of the stars, the Sun and Moon were of grand importance to our ancestors. By understanding the Hermetic Maxim of "As above, so below," we can understand the importance of time-keeping for following the cycles of the heavens was to be following the cycles *inside of you*. The heavens reflected the motions within the self, and staying in time with those motions allowed the harmony of the universe to guide oneself on one's journey. The Moon, Sun and stars are heavenly bodies whose attributes and powers exist *hidden* within oneself, just like the calendars *hidden* within chess. Chess is truly a nobleman's game and has withstood the test of time. There is good reason why, because the game of chess is crafted with three languages, words, symbols and numbers. By synthesizing these three languages, chess remains one of the most fascinating games of the ages. And its creators were not done with us yet. Apparently, they wanted to remind us one more time about that holy, transcendental number of Pi.

By reducing down the characters of our board to decimal parity, or digital root, we can calculate a whole number approximation of Pi. Shown below is one side of the board. Since we know each Pawn actually encodes Pi and is the only character on the board who doesn't need to be reduced down by decimal parity (since *Pawn* already equals 9), we can delineate the pawn with our Pi symbol.

12	29	24	16	21	24	29	12
9	9	9	9	9	9	9	9

Numerical Equivalent

3	2	6	7	3	6	2	3
π	π	π	π	π	π	π	π

Decimal Parity Reduction

By connecting the branches of our menorah and dividing by the 7 of the King, *leaving only the mighty 3* represented by the *Queen*, we can derive Pi. What is most interesting is that before the reduction, *Queen* summed to **21**. **21** divided by its reduction, or 3 gives us once again the **7** we need to derive Pi. The craftmanship of chess is truly astonishing.

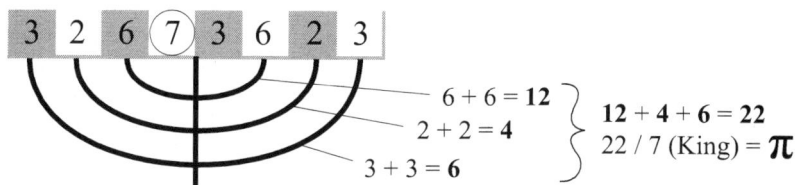

| 3 | 2 | 6 | (7) | 3 | 6 | 2 | 3 |

$6 + 6 = 12$
$2 + 2 = 4$
$3 + 3 = 6$

$12 + 4 + 6 = 22$
$22 / 7 \ (\text{King}) = \pi$

Chess is a game that is most often played in silence. The only time a word is usually spoken is when a player says *check* or *checkmate*. By using our decimal parity reduction and subtracting the numbers across the top of the board, starting from either left to right or right to left, it yields us the number **-26**.

3	2	6	7	3	6	2	3

$$3 - 2 - 6 - 7 - 3 - 6 - 2 - 3 = -26$$

26 represents the number of characters in our alphabet and since speaking is usually prohibited during the game, it is most interesting that subtracting our royalty yields us a negative **26**.

Before we move on, let's take one last look at the *King*. Since toppling the opponent's *King* is the ultimate goal of the game, the *King* has an added importance. The multiplication of the numerical equivalent of the *King* yields us the number **105**.

KING
3 5 1 7

$$3 \times 5 \times 1 \times 7 = 105$$

The entire game of chess can be played with one hand, for it only takes one hand to move a piece and you are only allowed to move one piece at a time. This fact comes in handy in trying to understand what the King is encoding. Since we have utilized our hands so much throughout this study, let's take a look at the 14 phalanges of our hand once again. By adding up the 14 sections of our hand, we yield the number **105**.

$$1 + 2 + 3 + 4 + 5 + 6 + 7 + 8 + 9 + 10 + 11 + 12 + 13 + 14 = 105$$

By the multiplication of King summing to **105** and the 14 sections of your 5 fingers, or 1 through 14, summing to **105**, the King in chess is actually telling you who the King in the game is.

And that would be, of course, *you*.

THE THRICE GREAT HERMES

Alchemy has its origins in Egypt, and many credit its birth to a man, most likely a mythological character, named the Thrice Great Hermes Trismegistus. Hermes was considered the "Master of the Masters" and supposedly brought the knowledge of writing, mathematics, astrology, geometry and gematria to the people of Earth. The remnants of the work of Hermes have been collected in such books as the *Kybalion*, *The Emerald Tablet of Hermes* and the *Corpus Hermeticum*. These texts are highly respected books in occult and esoteric circles, and provide a wealth of wisdom rich in poetic symbolism and philosophical prose.

No matter if Hermes was a real man or not, Hermes Trismegistus is an archetype like Christ, Buddha and the kabalistic Adam Kadmon that represented the spiritually ascended man, the man who rose from the lower animal self and climbed the rungs of the ladder to his higher, awakened self. It was the archetype of he recognizing the god within and without. Understanding the working principles of the universe was quintessential to achieving this enlightened state. Seven Hermetic principles were named, upon which the entire Hermetic Philosophy is based. They are as follows:

1. The Principle of Mentalism -
    "The ALL IS MIND; the Universe is Mental."
2. The Principle of Correspondence -
    "As above so below; as below so above."
3. The Principle of Vibration -
    "Nothing rests; everything moves; everything vibrates."
4. The Principle of Polarity -
    "Everything is Dual; everything has its pair of opposites; all
    paradoxes may be reconciled."
5. The Principle of Rhythm -
    "Everything flows, out and in; everything has its tides; all things
    rise and fall."
6. The Principle of Cause and Effect -
    "Every Cause has its Effect; every Effect has its Cause; everything
    happens according to Law."
7. The Principle of Gender -
    "Gender is in everything; everything has its Masculine and Feminine
    Princples."

Hermes was named "Thrice Great", which is no doubt a reference to the power of the Holy Trinity and our holy Pi. Much like the holy name of Jesus Christ that we saw in Volume 1, the holy name of Hermes Trismegistus has much to offer us as well. Understanding the numerology behind these characters' names helps elucidate core philosophical and occult truths embodied within. The aura and magic surrounding these enlightened characters has captivated people through the ages, and this not simply the result of religious fervor and idol worship. Inherent universal truths were purposefully crafted into the names and stories of these gods, done so for the sole purpose that one day we might lift the veil of our ignorance and bask at the glory of their wisdom. Names with numbers and letters coming together in the most well crafted way to tell the most profound story of all - *the story of the god who dwells within.*

The holy name of the Thrice Great Hermes Trismegistus, no matter how we look at it, will invariably lead us back to *our own two hands.*

$$\underbrace{\text{HERMES}}_{28} \underbrace{\text{TRISMEGISTUS}}_{66} = 94$$

$$6\,5\,5\,1\,5\,6 \quad 7\,5\,5\,6\,1\,5\,7\,5\,6\,7\,6\,6 = 94$$

We know, like *Thoth, Holy Bible, Liberty,* and *Freedom, Hermes* sums to **28**, representing the phalanges of our two hands. If we assign the phalanges of our fingers 1-14 (making 13 and 14, or Pi our thumb) and use decimal parity on each finger, we will end up with **6** on each finger and **9** on our thumb, summing to **33!**

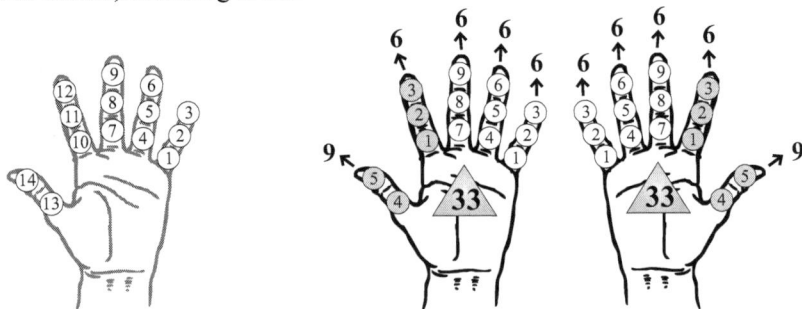

Assigning 1 - 14

Decimal Parity Equivalent
$6 + 6 + 6 + 6 + 9 = 33$

Joining our hands in the act of prayer would then give us two numbers **28** and **66**, or Hermes (**28**) Trismegistus (**66**).

Hermes was no doubt a master craftsman with a *square* and *compass*. The mirror of **94** yields us **49** which is the numerical equivalent of Compass and Square as well as our holy number 7 squared (7 x 7 = **49**).

HERMES TRISMEGISTUS   COMPASS SQUARE
6 5 5 1 5 6   7 5 5 6 1 5 7 5 6 7 6 6 = **94** **49** = 3 2 1 3 1 6 6 + 6 4 6 1 5 5

Dividing Hermes Trismegistus by 2 yields us two **47**s (94 / 2 = **47**) - representing Heaven and Earth in *numbers* as well as *letters*.

THREE   FOUR   HEAVEN   EARTH
7 6 5 5 5 +   6 2 6 5 = **47**   6 5 1 5 5 1 +   5 1 5 7 6 = **47**

In order to understand the importance of Hermes' name even further, we are going to need some help from the Egyptian alphabet. We split our alphabet, making 13 letters per side and resting on the letters **G** and **T**. The letters **G** and **T** in the Egyptian alphabet are interesting glyphs. The **G** is a vessel or pot that has a triangle resting in it, and the glyph for **T** is a semi-circle and a tear drop (see Egyptian Alphabet - Helpful Resources). This *Triangle* and *Tear Drop* give us not only the 32 and 33 degrees of Scottish Rite Freemasonry, but they also reference the 360 degrees of a circle. The interior angles of the Triangle equal 180 degrees, and the semi-circle equals 180 degrees as well, combing to give us the 360 degrees of a circle.

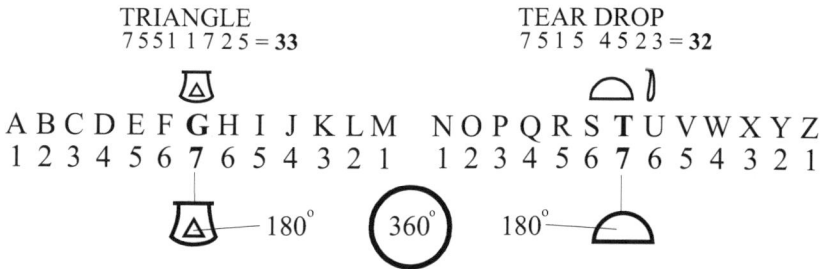

TRIANGLE   TEAR DROP
7 5 5 1 1 7 2 5 = **33**   7 5 1 5   4 5 2 3 = **32**

A	B	C	D	E	F	G	H	I	J	K	L	M		N	O	P	Q	R	S	T	U	V	W	X	Y	Z
1	2	3	4	5	6	7	6	5	4	3	2	1		1	2	3	4	5	6	7	6	5	4	3	2	1

We can also find this 360 degrees of a circle by mirroring our number line of 0-9, something we will explore in just a bit. By mirroring our number line, we get a symmetrical set of numbers that allows us to see both the Yin / Yang, Shiva / Shakti or Adam / Eve principles within our Ennead. Hermes performed the alchemical marriage on himself and married these opposite forces that lay divided within. This is where the term *hermetic-ally sealed* is derived. A hermetic seal is taking two opposites and merging them so tightly they become one. They are a **sealed**, *unified being*.

90

We know that adding the numerical equivalents of *zero* through *nine* will yield us the number 180. Henceforth, if we mirror our 0-9 this would provide us with the 360 degrees of a circle. Unifying the zeroes would also give us one of the most fundamental geometric forms of creation, the Vesica Piscis.

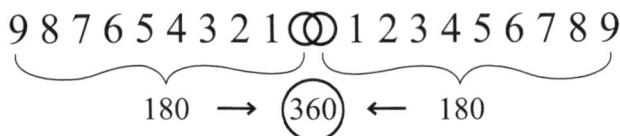

$$9\ 8\ 7\ 6\ 5\ 4\ 3\ 2\ 1\ \text{①}\ 1\ 2\ 3\ 4\ 5\ 6\ 7\ 8\ 9$$

$$180 \longrightarrow (360) \longleftarrow 180$$

We understand that multiplying the numbers 1 - 7 will give us the combined radius of the Earth and Moon known as Squaring the Circle. Since we now have 1 through 7 twice, this would find us the diameters of both the Earth and Moon combined, being **10,080** miles. It would seem that our entire number line is dealing with that ancient magical art of Squaring the Circle for even 8 and 9 reference the art as well. The area of a circle with 9 will approximately equal the area of a square of 8. Since our 8 and 9 are mirrored, we can view this art as Squaring the Circle or Circling the Square, which using our cipher, not coincidentally, both sum to **76**, or the angle of the missing capstone on the Great Pyramid.

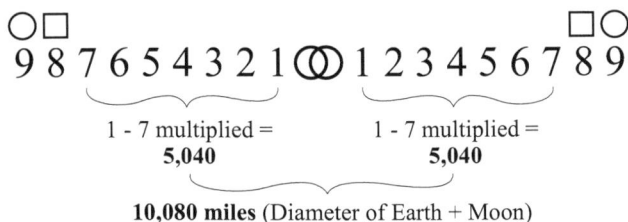

○□   □○
$$9\ 8\ 7\ 6\ 5\ 4\ 3\ 2\ 1\ \text{①}\ 1\ 2\ 3\ 4\ 5\ 6\ 7\ 8\ 9$$

1 - 7 multiplied =   1 - 7 multiplied =
5,040   **5,040**

10,080 miles (Diameter of Earth + Moon)

SQUARING THE CIRCLE
6 4 6 15 5 1 7 7 6 5 3 5 5 3 2 5 = **76**

CIRCLING THE SQUARE
3 5 5 3 2 5 1 7 7 6 5 6 4 6 1 5 5 = **76**

⋀ Circle of ⑨ : $\pi \times 4.5^2 \simeq 63.63$

⋁ Square of ⑧ : $8^2 = 64$

Adding 1-7 yields us **28** twice, representative of the hands of Adam and the hands of Eve, the eternal opposites within the self with each hand given the tools of either the compass or the square, being **8** and **9** respectively.

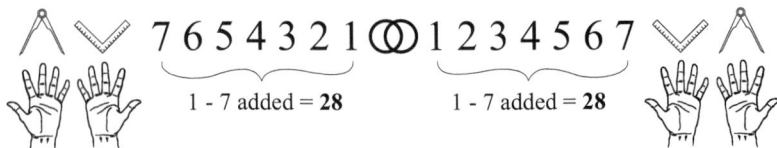

⋀ ⋁ $7\ 6\ 5\ 4\ 3\ 2\ 1\ \text{①}\ 1\ 2\ 3\ 4\ 5\ 6\ 7$ ⋁ ⋀

1 - 7 added = **28**   1 - 7 added = **28**

Now that we have de-constructed our number line, let us put our mirrored 0-9 inside the 360 degrees of a circle to represent the *first circle in existence.* We can use the Seal of Solomon or Star of David to symbolize this first circle. The 180 degrees of each of the triangles, one pointing above and one pointing below, represent 0-9 or the 180 we find with the numerical equivalents of the words *zero - nine.* In Volume 1 we found the Holy 108 of Phi as well as the Hermetic Seal within this symbol (see chapter The Golden Proportion, Vol. 1). Here again, this holy alchemical, Hermetic, and Jewish symbol gives us insights into the beginnings of our creation.

"So below"
0 1 2 3 4 5 6 7 8 9
Zero - Nine = **180**
180 Degrees

"As above"
0 1 2 3 4 5 6 7 8 9
Zero - Nine = **180**
180 Degrees

Adding the digits 1- 9 sums to **45** ($1 + 2 + 3 + 4 + 5 + 6 + 7 + 8 + 9 = 45$). Since we have two sets of these digits inside the Star of David, this gives us a total of **90,** representing the **90** degrees of the *first right angle in existence.* We can find this **90** in the second Hermetic Principle, or the Principle of Correspondence, known by the infamous alchemical phrase: "As above so below; as below so above."

AS ABOVE, SO BELOW
1 6 1 2 2 5 5   6 2 2 5 2 2 4

AS BELOW, SO ABOVE
1 6 2 5 2 2 4   6 2 1 2 2 5 5

90^0

45 → (**90**) ← **45**

With our Seal of Solomon now representing our *first circle and first right angle in existence,* we can continue to walk up the number line, mirroring the numbers as we climb. Since we are dealing with the Thrice Great Hermes, let's focus on the next three numbers - 10, 11, 12 and and their mirrors 01, 11 and 21. Notice both 10, 11, and 12 as well as 01, 11, and 21 sum to **33,** representing the decimal parity equivalent of each of your hands and the numerical equivalent of *Trismegistus.*

(21, 11, 01)
21 + 11 + 01 =
33

(10, 11, 12)
10 + 11 + 12 =
33

TRISMEGISTUS
7 5 5 6 1 5 7 5 6 7 6 6 = **66**

Walking up to **13** and **31** in our number line finds us establishing the decimal place in Pi (...**13**.1415). Let's focus on the eight numbers walking out of our Seal of Solomon (10, 11, 12, 13 and 01, 11, 21, 31). If we find the numerical equivalents for each of these words the most astonishing correspondence occurs. Both sides sum to a total of **105**. This would bring the total of these eight numbers to be **210**, and this **210** is yet another reference to your two hands. Once again, as we did in the game of chess, adding 1-14, or totaling the phalanges of your hand, equals **105**. Therefore, your two hands would sum to **210!** All of this is embedded in the very numbers we use and words we speak.

.31 (21, 11, 01) ✡ (10, 11, 12) 13.

ONE
8 = 2 1 5
ELEVEN
23 = 5 2 5 5 5 1
TWENTY ONE
34 = 7 4 5 1 7 2 2 1 5
THIRTY ONE
40 = 7 6 5 5 7 2 2 1 5

TEN
7 5 1 = 13
ELEVEN
5 2 5 5 5 1 = 23
TWELVE
7 4 5 2 5 5 = 28
THIRTEEN
7 6 5 5 7 5 5 1 = 41

Adding
1 - 14 =
105

Adding
1 - 14 =
105

105 → 210 ← 105

(8 + 23 + 34 + 40)   (13 + 23 + 28 + 41)

We will continue walking up the number line to find the Cross of Christ in the next chapter, but for now, let's take a further look at your two hands. The Great Trinity in Heaven has expressed its thrice greatness in the craftiest of ways on Earth. The numerical equivalents of *Three, Six, Nine* (*which references 12*) and *Twelve, all divisible by three,* want to tell you about the *handy* work of the Great Trinity. Catching the knowledge of the trinity in the *vessel of the human being* is the recognized in the Egyptian letter **G** and in the symbol of the Freemasons. *God is no further than before your very eyes and right on your two hands.*

THREE
7 6 5 5 5 = **28**
SIX
6 5 3 = **14**
NINE
1 5 1 5 = **12**
TWELVE
7 4 5 2 5 5 = **28**

THE CROSS OF CHRIST

The life and ministry of Jesus Christ has captivated the hearts, minds, and souls of people for centuries. Adoration and love for Christ reaches every corner of the world. Jesus Christ, the man, has been given so many distinctions; he was a preacher, prophet, sage, magician, philosopher, healer, and Messiah. The sacred object, or talisman, that is attributed to Christ, as we all know, is the cross. In Volume 1 we discovered that the numerical equivalent and geometry of the cross encodes Pi and the cross itself actually reveals to us the magical geometry at work in our sky. Jesus's death came by way of the cross, and his crucifixion or *Passion* was divided into **14** stations or *Ways of the Cross* before his ultimate death and resurrection. This number **14** is where we found the decimal place in Pi established in our number line, and this number and its mirror, 41, will serve as a focal point for understanding the numerical aspects of the myth of Jesus and the cross.

We saw in the last chapter that the mirrors of 0-9 can be placed inside the 360 degrees of a circle we symbolized as the Seal of Solomon. This Jewish symbol will work well as we continue forward since Jesus himself was of Jewish descent. In Volume 1, in the chapter entitled "The Garden of Even" we delineated 01 to be Adam and 10 to be Eve, making Adam and Eve reflections of each other.

Adam - 01 ✡ 10 - Eve

Since Adam and Eve were cast out of the Garden of Eden, let's remove the 01 and 10 and continue to walk up our number line, mirroring the numbers as we go along. To review, we can square the numbers 11, 12 and 13 and 11, 21, and 31, and they will mirror each other perfectly up to the number 14 and 41, or where the decimal place is established in Pi.

$$11^2 = 121 \qquad 121 = 11^2$$
$$12^2 = 144 \qquad 441 = 21^2$$
$$13^2 = 169 \qquad 961 = 31^2$$

This place between **13** and **14** in our number line has been the focal point for so many of our myths and, as we will see, in constructing the cross, using numbers, letters, and mirrors, this **13** and **14** are no different.

By starting at the numbers 11 | 11, we can continue all the way up to the number 19 and 91, mirroring the numbers as we go along, finding the numerical equivalents for the words of each number. We will stop at 19 and 91 for several reasons. 19 is the square root of that all-powerful number of the Monad, 361. 91, when placed around the four ninety degree angles of a cross, gives us the **364**-day calendar seen in the Mayan Chichen Itza pyramid and the deck of cards (adding 1-13 = 91 x 4 suits = **364**).

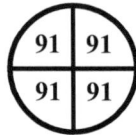

$$\sqrt{361} = 19$$

By climbing up the number line from 11 to 19, the most magical correspondence happens between numbers and letters. The *difference* between the numerical equivalents of the words and their mirrors are listed running down the fulcrum of the cross with SEVEN (equivalent to Pi) being the axis point, or the arms of the cross represented by **14** and **41** recognized by the *14 Stations of the Cross*. The symbol of the cross gives us a beautiful way to express this linguistic and mathematic correlation.

91, 81, 71, 61, 51, 41 .31 21, 11, <u>01</u> ✡ <u>10</u>, 11, 12, 13. 14, 15, 16, 17, 18, 19

ELEVEN 5 2 5 5 5 1 = **23**	**(0)**	ELEVEN **23** = 5 2 5 5 5 1
TWELVE 7 4 5 2 5 5 = **28**	**(6)**	TWENTY ONE **34** = 7 4 5 1 7 2 2 1 5
THIRTEEN 7 6 5 5 7 5 5 1 = **41**	**(1)**	THIRTY ONE **40** = 7 6 5 5 7 2 2 1 5
FOURTEEN 6 2 6 5 7 5 5 1 = **37**	**π**	FORTY ONE **30** = 6 2 5 7 2 2 1 5
FIFTEEN 6 5 6 7 5 5 1 = **35**	**(1)**	FIFTY ONE **34** = 6 5 6 7 2 2 1 5
SIXTEEN 6 5 3 7 5 5 1 = **32**	**(1)**	SIXTY ONE **31** = 6 5 3 7 2 2 1 5
SEVENTEEN 6 5 5 5 1 7 5 5 1 = **40**	**(1)**	SEVENTY ONE **39** = 6 5 5 5 1 7 2 2 1 5
EIGHTEEN 5 5 7 6 7 5 5 1 = **41**	**(1)**	EIGHTY ONE **40** = 5 5 7 6 7 2 2 1 5
NINETEEN 1 5 1 5 7 5 5 1 = **30**	**(1)**	NINETY ONE **29** = 1 5 1 5 7 2 2 1 5

The wisdom behind the cross runs deep. Explore the cross yourself for it has much to offer. Some key elements are elucidated on the following page.

"So below"
0 1 2 3 4 5 6 7 8 9
Zero - Nine = **180**
180 Degrees

01
Adam

"As above"
0 1 2 3 4 5 6 7 8 9
Zero - Nine = **180**
180 Degrees

10
Eve

ELEVEN
5 2 5 5 5 1 = **23**

ELEVEN
23 = 5 2 5 5 5 1

TWELVE
7 4 5 2 5 5 = **28**

TWENTY ONE
34 = 7 4 5 1 7 2 2 1 5

THIRTEEN
7 6 5 5 7 5 5 1 = **41**

THIRTY ONE
40 = 7 6 5 5 7 2 2 1 5

FOURTEEN
6 2 6 5 7 5 5 1 = **37**

π

FORTY ONE
30 = 6 2 5 7 2 2 1 5

FIFTEEN
6 5 6 7 5 5 1 = **35**

FIFTY ONE
34 = 6 5 6 7 2 2 1 5

SIXTEEN
6 5 3 7 5 5 1 = **32**

SIXTY ONE
31 = 6 5 3 7 2 2 1 5

SEVENTEEN
6 5 5 5 1 7 5 5 1 = **40**

SEVENTY ONE
39 = 6 5 5 5 1 7 2 2 1 5

EIGHTEEN
5 5 7 6 7 5 5 1 = **41**

EIGHTY ONE
40 = 5 5 7 6 7 2 2 1 5

NINETEEN
1 5 1 5 7 5 5 1 = **30**

NINETY ONE
29 = 1 5 1 5 7 2 2 1 5

☥ The Egyptian Ankh, called the Crux Ansanta, perfectly fits in the motif underlain as shown above.

Adding the numbers down the fulcrum of the cross (0 + 1 + 6 + 7 + 1 + 1 + 1 + 1 + 1) sums to **19**, the square root of the Monad. Adding 1-19 sums to **190** (a number that we will explore in depth in the chapter entitled "Genesis 1:1"). Notice under the arms of the cross, the difference between the numerical equivalents of the words *is always one.*

Adding the sums of *Fourteen* and *Forty-one*, or the arms of our cross, equals **67**, the numerical equivalent of *All-Seeing Eye of God* and most importantly *Keeper of the Balance.* Its mirror being **76.**

Adding the 10 numbers under the arms of the cross (35 + 34 + 32 + 31 + 40 + 39 + 41 + 40 + 30 + 29) sums to **351.** Adding 1-26 sums to **351.** The mirror of 351 is 153, (We will explore this numerical relationship in depth in the chapter entitled "153 and the Ark in Scripture.")

THE 12 DISCIPLES OF THE ZODIAC

The ministry of Jesus Christ is the focal point of the New Testament, and Jesus himself is the Savior of the Christian religion. This Sun of God was infamous for healing the sick, for the miracles he performed, and most importantly that he died for our sins. People the world over adore, pray to, and worship Jesus, the man, every single day, yet little do they know that Jesus Christ, the archetypal figure, and his twelve disciples are a beautifully crafted metaphor for the sun and the 12 ages of the zodiac that the sun passes through in its journey across our skies throughout the year.

In Volume 1 we explored the numerology of the holy name of Jesus Christ and found that not only does his name encode the Ennead within the wise number 666, the diameter of the sun in miles, the number of days in the solar year, the 32 degrees of Freemasonic ascension, and the 59 beads in a traditional Christian rosary, but it also encodes the 18 years missing in the account of his life. The numerical breakdown of the name Jesus Christ is once again abridged below.

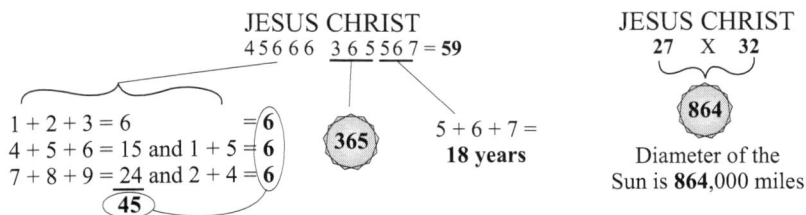

JESUS CHRIST
4 5 6 6 6   3 6 5 5 6 7 = **59**

$1 + 2 + 3 = 6$ = **6**
$4 + 5 + 6 = 15$ and $1 + 5 = $ **6**
$7 + 8 + 9 = 24$ and $2 + 4 = $ **6**
45

365

$5 + 6 + 7 = $ **18 years**

JESUS CHRIST
27   X   **32**

864

Diameter of the
Sun is **864**,000 miles

The 18 years in the account of Jesus' life missing from the Bible are seen in the IST within the title Christ. Jesus went missing at age 12. This would mean that after 18 years, Jesus realized his divine nature and started his ministry at age 30. The story of Jesus' illumination, not even mentioned in the bible and left to the reader's imagination, gives us two very important numbers to work with, **12** and **30**. Not coincidentally, there are **12** ages in the zodiac, and each age is represented by **30** degrees of a circle. When Jesus began his ministry, he carried with him twelve disciples which is yet again another reference to the 12 houses or ages of the zodiac. These 12 disciples listed in Acts 1:13 of the King James Bible are as follows:

And when they had entered, they went up to the upper room, where they were staying, **Peter** and **John** and **James** and **Andrew**, **Philip** and **Thomas**, **Bartholomew** and **Matthew**, **James** the son of Alphaeus and **Simon** the Zealot and **Judas** the son of James.

97

The only disciple not listed in this verse is Judas Iscariot. Judas was one of the original 12 disciples until he betrayed Jesus by informing the Sanhedrin priests of Jesus' whereabouts. The infamous *Kiss of Judas* is a significant biblical story whose meaning is often disputed amongst biblical scholars. The term *selling out*, or losing one's integrity, is said to be derived from this event. Judas Iscariot *sold Jesus out* for a mere 30 pieces of silver, to which he then bought a parcel of land. After significant guilt and remorse over his wrong-doing, Judas committed suicide by hanging himself. The 30 pieces of silver obtained by Judas is recognized as a metaphor for the 30 degrees of the zodiac to which he was originally a part of. The land he bought by removing himself from the heavenly circle of the zodiac was a moral allegory identifying his greatest sin. Judas sold out the Christ, *or great spirit within him*, sacrificing his slice of heaven (or his 30 degrees of the zodiac) for the earthly possessions of land and silver. It is one of the greatest stories of recognizing the futility of yearning for material wealth.

Taking the place of Judas Iscariot to complete the 12 ages of the zodiac and the 12 disciples of Christ (completing our *12 around 1* - making for our ever-recurring, all-important number **13**) was Matthias. Understanding that the 12 disciples of Christ is nothing more than an allegory for the 12 ages of our zodiac, we are able to assign each disciple to each of the 12 houses, with Jesus Christ, the Sun of God, sitting at his rightful throne in the center of our 12 spoked wheel in the heavens. The particular houses we may assign to each disciple is still in question, and many astrologers might disagree with this correlation and placement - either way this will not effect our numerical study. Further examination of the characters and stories pertaining to these disciples is highly recommended.

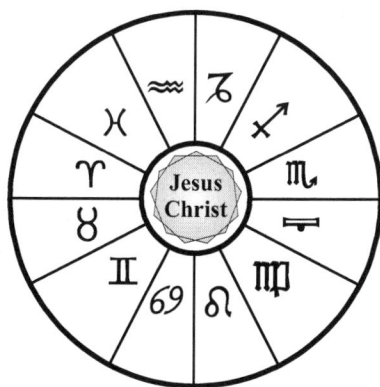

♈	Aries = Thomas
♉	Taurus = Matthias
♊	Gemini = Judas
♋	Cancer = Matthew
♌	Leo = Simon
♍	Virgo = Bartholomew
♎	Libra = Peter
♏	Scorpio = Andrew
♐	Sagittarius = James
♑	Capricorn = John
♒	Aquarius = James
♓	Piscis = Philip

The numerical equivalents for the 12 disciples of Christ are listed below.

ANDREW
1 1 4 5 5 4 = **20**

MATTHEW
1 1 7 7 6 5 4 = **31**

JOHN
4 2 6 1 = **13**

THOMAS
7 6 2 1 1 6 = **23**

JAMES
4 1 1 5 6 = **17**

JUDAS
4 6 4 1 6 = **21**

JAMES
4 1 1 5 6 = **17**

BARTHOLOMEW
2 1 5 7 6 2 2 2 1 5 4 = **37**

PHILIP
3 6 5 2 5 3 = **24**

SIMON
6 5 1 2 1 = **15**

PETER
3 5 7 5 5 = **25**

MATTHIAS
1 1 7 7 6 5 1 6 = **34**

Adding the numerical equivalent of the holy name of Jesus Christ, **59**, to his 12 disciples sums to the number **336** (20 + 31 + 13 + 23 + 17 + 21 + 17 + 37 + 24 + 15 + 25 + 34 + 59 = **336**). We saw this number **336** in two chapters thus far, "The Alchemical Marriage" and "Chess", with the multiplication of the King and Queen summing to **336**. Through the 16 of the King and the 21 of the Queen, we were able to establish the **365** day solar year within our number line. Since we are dealing with the 12 months that the sun passes through in our year on Earth, it should come as no surprise that we find this mighty **336** in the 12 disciples of Christ.

♈ = Thomas
♉ = Matthias
♊ = Judas
♋ = Matthew
♌ = Simon
♍ = Bartholomew

♎ = Peter
♏ = Andrew
♐ = James
♑ = John
♒ = James
♓ = Philip

† Jesus Christ } **336**

16 17 18 19 20 **21**

16 x 21 = **336**
1 + 7 + 1 + 8 +
1 + 9 + 2 + 0 = **29**

} **365**

The four alchemical elements, *Earth, Air, Water* and *Fire* were often paired with a transcendental element called *Aether*. *Aether* was the element that existed within the spiritual world and was often considered to merely effect the natural 4 elements we experience on the material plane. Adding the numerical equivalent of *Aether* to the 78 of Earth, Air, Water and Fire, sums to **107**.

EARTH
5 1 5 7 6

WATER
4 1 7 5 5

AIR
1 5 5

FIRE
6 5 5 5

AETHER
1 5 7 6 5 5

} **107**

The six colors of the Olympic flag as well as *The United States of America* both sum to **107** with **107** being the 28th prime number. **107** multiplied by Pi equals **336** (107 x 3.14 = **336**).

How does the **336** of the twelve disciples and Christ correlate to the **315** of the 12 ages of the zodiac? We will leave that to your imagination - just remember, make sure to count the *fire* of spirit *within yourself.*

HORUS THE SUN GOD

The Egyptian falcon-headed god Horus is one of the most well-known and significant deities in the Egyptian pantheon. Horus is akin to Jesus and is the son of the gods Isis and Osiris after Osiris was dismembered by Isis's brother Set. Horus and Set have been in battle ever since, and this mythological cosmic drama is played out every day in our skies. Horus rises and Set sets him everyday. Horus is yet another character, an anthropomorphized Sun god whose name is a treasure trove of sacred geometrical and mathematical goodies.

Horus rises and sets everyday on the *Horizon*. *Horus rising* is in fact where the term horizon stems from (the "izon" in horizon being an anagram for the holy Mount *Zion*, a sacred hill in Jerusalem). We saw in Volume 1 that "Horizon" encodes Pi, and the horizon itself can be used as the diameter to find the circumference of the sun, shown again below.

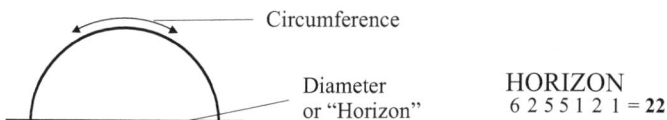

HORIZON
6 2 5 5 1 2 1 = **22**

Notice that when Horus rises, it's the morning. *Morning* itself sums to 22 and has seven letters. 22 divided by the 7 letters of *morning* yields us Pi once again.

MORNING
1 2 5 1 51 7 = **22**

The numerical equivalents of the letters of Horus are shown below. Before we simply add these numbers across to find the sum of Horus, let's first multiply these numbers and see what our Sun god has in store.

HORUS
6 2 5 66

$6 \times 2 \times 5 \times 6 \times 6 = \boxed{2,160}$

With the multiplication of Horus summing to **2,160,** the alchemical marriage of the eternal opposites of the Sun and the Moon cryptically reside in the beautiful and simple numerology of this great Egyptian god. The diameter of the Moon is **2,160** miles, and there are 12 zodiacal ages through which the sun precesses with each age being **2,160** years. The fact that both distance and time can be understood easily by understanding the power of a number such as **2,160** speaks volumes about the architecture of our universe. Simple number patterns, geometry, and a few basic laws construct our ever-complexifing world. Intuiting and comprehending these basic principles initiates one into a world of synchronicity, beauty, and holistic understanding.

The **2,160** we obtain with the multiplication of Horus can be found in three other very interesting places. The first is in the measurement of arc minutes. The arc minute is a unit of angular measurement used in cartography and navigation equal to 1/60th of one degree (with 60 arc-seconds in each arc minute). Since there are 360 degrees in a circle, the meridian circumference of the Earth is defined as 21,600 arc minutes (60 arc minutes x 360 degrees of a circle = 21,600). 21,600 is simply **2,160** multiplied by ten.

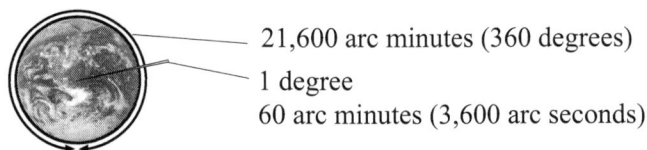

21,600 arc minutes (360 degrees)

1 degree

60 arc minutes (3,600 arc seconds)

The second place we can find this **2,160** is in the cube, one of the Platonic solids. We have seen the power of this cube as the focus of the Islamic Hajj pilgrimage as well as in the ancient art of *Doubling the Cube.* When we unfold our cube from 3 dimensions to 2, it will naturally create a cross as shown below. It should be no surprise that Horus, being akin to Jesus (and Jesus being intrinsically connected to the sign of the cross), that we find this sacred symbol within the numerology of the sun god Horus. Each square on cross/cube has four 90 degree corners making for a total of 360 degrees per square. 360 x the 6 squares equals **2,160.**

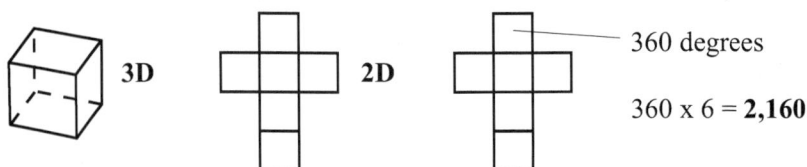

3D

2D

360 degrees

360 x 6 = **2,160**

The last place that we will locate our 2,160 is, yet again, in the cube. Making the sides of the cube a length of 6 units each will make the total volume of the cube **216** units, which is of course nothing more than a division of 10 from our 2,160. Also notice, this also establishes our cube as being **666**.

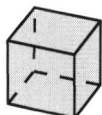

Each side = Unit of 6
6 x 6 x 6 = **216** (6 cubed)

The Magic Square of the sun (a square being nothing more than a cube in 2 dimensions) is the numbers 1-36. When added together they sum to **666**. Magic Squares are squares that contain particular numbers arranged in equal rows and columns, such that the sum of each row, column, and sometimes diagonal are the same. The Magic Square of the Sun is shown below as well as its decimal parity reduction equivalent. Notice that on the Magic Square of the Sun, each row sums to **111** - the same as the numerical equivalent of *Omnipotent, Omniscient, Omnipresent, And God said, Let there be Light, Hear No Evil, See No Evil, Speak No Evil*, as well as the sum of the addition of the 6 pieces in the game of chess (*Pawn, Rook, Knight, Bishop, Queen,* and *King*). Adding the decimal parity equivalent, each row sums to 30 with the total square equaling **180**, or half a Pi!

Standard

6	32	3	34	35	1
7	11	27	28	8	30
19	14	16	15	23	24
18	20	22	21	17	13
25	29	10	9	26	12
36	5	33	4	2	31

Each row sums to **111**
6 rows x 111 = **666**

Decimal Parity Equivalent

6	5	3	7	8	1
7	2	9	1	8	3
1	5	7	6	5	6
9	2	4	3	8	4
7	2	1	9	8	3
9	5	6	4	2	4

Each row sums to **30**
6 rows x 30 = **180**

The construction of Magic Squares must be done with precision since the misplacement of any single number will throw the entire square off. Magic Squares have been known since antiquity and are seen all over the world from Persia to China to India. The Magic Square of the Sun - or better stated, *The Magic Square of Horus* - is definitely one of the most famous for the simple genius in its construction is truly unparalleled.

The holy name of Horus has much more in store for us. The regular addition of the numerical equivalent of Horus yields us the number **25**.

HORUS
6 2 5 6 6 = **25**

If we separate the **5** letters in the word Horus into HOR and US, breaking it up syllabically (hor-us), we find the numbers **13** and **12**. Horus sums to **25**, with the square root of **25** being **5**.

HOR   US
6 2 5   6 6 = $\sqrt{25}$ = **5**
(13)   (12)

By focusing on these three numbers, **5**, **12**, and **13**, cryptically encoded within the numerology, it allows to perform an alchemical marriage and find the Moon within our Sun God. In Volume 1 we looked at the **5, 12**, and **13** Pythagorean or *lunation triangle,* and how this triangle, used at Stonehenge, gives us a way to map the lunar year to the solar year. By drawing a line from the triangle's corner to its adjacent side, separating it by 2 and 3, this line will measure **12.369**, which is the square root of 153 (a number we will explore in the next chapter). Multiplying this number by the 29.53 days of a Lunar month, yields the number of days of our solar year.

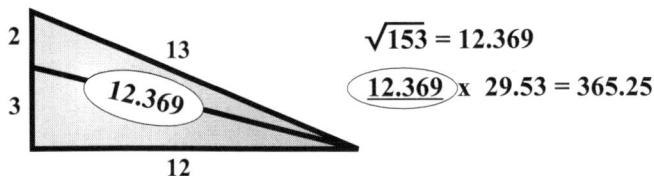

$\sqrt{153} = 12.369$

$12.369 \times 29.53 = 365.25$

Dividing the adjacent side of the triangle into 2 and 3, as we did in the name of Horus, also resonates with the Major and Minor keys of the piano. Notice that there are 12 notes of the chromatic scale, the 13th being the octave with the Minor keys broken up into **2** and **3**.

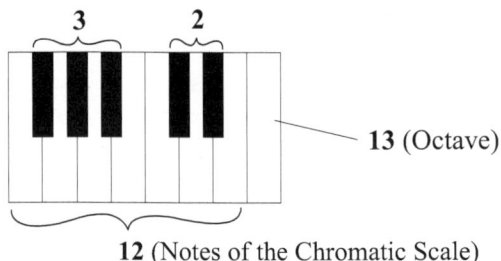

13 (Octave)

12 (Notes of the Chromatic Scale)

Since the name of Horus encodes numbers for both itself, the Sun, as well as the Moon, we should assume that Horus also wants to tell us about time. In staying with the separation of the letters of Horus we can multiply the HOR and find the number 60 and leave the US, adding to 12, giving us the numbers we need to find the seconds in a minute, the minutes in an hour and the number of hours in a half day, all creatively and cleverly encoded within the great name of this Egyptian Sun God.

$$\begin{array}{cc} \times & + \\ \text{HOR} & \text{US} \\ 6\ 2\ 5 & 6\ 6 \\ \underbrace{\ \ } & \underbrace{\ \ } \\ \boxed{60} & \boxed{12} \end{array}$$

12 hours in a half day
60 seconds in a minute
60 minutes in an hour

Horus was also known as Ra and his antithesis was Set. The sum of Ra is **6** and the sum of Set is **18**, together giving us the 24 hours in one day. It is important to note that Ra gives us the numbers **5** and **1**, which we can view numerologically as the number **51**. We've seen the importance of this number time and time again and here again it shows its face in our Egyptian sun god. Lest we not forget that Ra's parents, *Isis* and *Osiris*, together sum to **51**!

$$\begin{array}{ccc} \text{RA} & \text{ISIS} & \text{OSIRIS} \\ \boxed{5\ 1} & 5656\ + & 2\ 65556 = \boxed{51} \end{array}$$

The first two words in Genesis 1:1 (a verse we will explore in depth later) are *In the*. Using our cipher, *In* gives us the numbers **5** and **1** and *The* yields us the numbers **765**. Notice that *In* is the identical numerical equivalent of *Ra* and the word *The* is nothing more than numerical anagram for *Set*.

$$\begin{array}{cc|cc} \text{RA} & \text{SET} & \text{IN} & \text{THE} \\ 5\ 1 & 6\ 57 & 5\ 1 & 7\ 6\ 5 \end{array}$$

Ra is the base of many words and names with mathematical and spiritual importance; **ra**ce, **ra**nge, **ra**ys, **ra**dius, **ra**diance, **ra**diate, **ra**inbow, **Ra**jah, **Ra**madan, Ab**ra**ham, **Ra**stafarian, etc. The not often used word ***Ra**dix* means "root, source, origin" and notice it almost seems to be the words *Ra* and *Six* put together. Not only does *Ra* sum to 6, but this source or origin also gives us the 6 directions of space with the 7th being the axis, which is, as we saw in Volume 1, nothing more than an anagram for *A Six*.

Ra is also a reference to the zodiacal sign of the Ram which is the head on the cosmological make-up of man.

With Ra, or Horus, being akin to Jesus, it should be no surprise that Jesus is recognized as the Lamb of God and Horus as the Ram. When the chrism, *or Christ fluid*, ascends up the spinal column and into the pineal gland, head or Ram, the individual is said to reach enlightenment and hence why the lamb or ram is placed on the head. Horus and Jesus, whether mythological characters or actual human beings, were said to have reached this heightened state of consciousness. We will explore this process further in the chapter entitled "The 3.5 of Pi."

Using the Hermetic Principle of Correspondence allows us to understand the allegories of our Sun gods a bit better. The path the sun takes through our skies, the rising and setting it does everyday is a reflection of our own lives. The journey we take through time, like all of nature, has ups and downs, ebbs and flows. In our lives we experience great joy and often great pain, and it is the balance of this light and dark, this Ra and Set, that keeps the entire universe spinning. Our entire life can be summed up in one day: our journey begins at the morning of our birth and ends at the death of our sunset. The Sun always *rising again*, is the powerfully inspirational message the sun reminds us of everyday and is the message one needs to intuit to help realize one's true potential. Every morning the Sun rises and wakes us up reminding us that we must indeed now "wake up" in our waking consciousness. And this *awakening*, this *enlightenment*, is knowing that the strength of the light of the sun is within you. With it, you can overcome any adversity. The first light of creation now exists as the soul within you. You are citizen of the cosmos, a child of God and a being of light. You are the *horizon* and the *diameter* needed to find the entire heavenly circle of the Sun. The limits of your own horizon rest entirely on your shoulders and, as we know, the power of God is on your two hands.

So the question is: *What's your next move?*

153 & THE ARK IN SCRIPTURE

The number 153 has been a mysterious number that has caught the eye of many biblical scholars. This specific number is mentioned in the Bible surrounding one of the miracles that Jesus performed. The reason for its specificity has plagued Bible readers for quite some time The miraculous draught, or catch of fish, is mentioned in the Bible twice with the number "an hundred and fifty and three" mentioned in the Gospel of St. John. Why would it be necessary to mention the exact number of fish Jesus caught? Is there perchance a deeper meaning behind this number? As we know from our studies, *everything has a deeper meaning.* As we will come to see, this miraculous number 153 is a number that has deep numerological, astronomical, and linguistic significance and becomes a vertex that can help us understand the archetypal and interconnected nature of all creation.

Below are the two places in the King James Bible in which the "miraculous draught of fish" are mentioned.

Luke 5:4-6 4) Now when he (Jesus) had left speaking, he said unto Simon, Launch out into the deep, and let down your nets for a draught. 5) And Simon answering said unto him, Master, we have toiled all the night, and have taken nothing: nevertheless at thy word I will let down the net. 6) And when they had this done, they inclosed a great multitude of fishes: and their net brake.

John 21: 5-11 5) Then Jesus saith unto them, Children, have ye any meat? They answered him, No. 6) And he said unto them, Cast the net on the right side of the ship, and ye shall find. They cast therefore, and now they were not able to draw it for the multitude of fishes. 7) Therefore that disciple whom Jesus loved saith unto Peter, It is the Lord. Now when Simon Peter heard that it was the Lord, he girt his fisher's coat unto him, (for he was naked,) and did cast himself into the sea. 8) And the other disciples came in a little ship; (for they were not far from land, but as it were two hundred cubits,) dragging the net with fishes. 9) As soon then as they were come to land, they saw a fire of coals there, and fish laid thereon, and bread. 10) Jesus saith unto them, Bring of the fish which ye have now caught. 11) Simon Peter went up, and drew the net to land full of great fishes, **an hundred and fifty and three**: and for all there were so many, yet was not the net broken.

Before we look into the number **153**, let's first focus on a particular aspect within the verse of St. John's Gospel. John 21:6 mentions that the fishermen must "Cast the net on the right side of the ship, and ye shall find." This is a most peculiar instruction from Jesus. Why would the fish they are to catch be swarming on merely the right side of the ship? The Bible deliberately presents information to us in this fashion to urge us to read between the lines, to look deeper within the story to find its true meaning. The right side of the ship in this instance is asking us to use our brains and think beyond the surface level of the story. In fact, the right side of the ship is nothing more than a reference to the *right side of your brain.*

The brain, like the Earth itself, is divided into two hemispheres. Each side of the brain lends itself to different modes or characteristics of thinking. The left side of the brain performs the more analytical functions while the right tends to lend itself to creative and artistic functions. Some of the characteristics we may assign to each side of the brain are listed below.

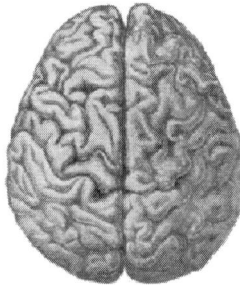

LOGICAL		CREATIVE
ANALYTICAL		IMAGINATIVE
SEQUENCING		HOLISTIC
LINEAR		INTUITIVE
MATHEMATICAL		NUMEROLOGICAL
LINGUISTIC		ARTISTIC
FACTUAL		RYTHMIC
COMPUTATIONAL		NON-VERBAL

Jesus telling his fishermen to cast their nets to the right side is merely him asking us to view the world in a creative fashion. He is asking us in fact to view the story of the 153 fish in a *creative way.* And in doing this, it will help us uncover the true meaning hidden beneath the story. It will also allow the reader to understand the creative nature of creation itself. Encoding messages like these in such a way allows us to peer into the absolute genius of these ancient religious writers. The Bible was not constructed by primitives or by people with superstitious minds. The Bible was written by people who understood the creative and hidden nature of God himself. Crafting stories in such a way allows the Holy Bible to encode fundamental truths of existence that withstand the test of time. These are stories that, when understood correctly, can relate to anyone, in any culture, on any continent, and in any aeon of time.

Now that we understand that the biblical writers wished for us to look at this story creatively, let's be creative with the number 153 itself. The first thing that we can do is mirror our 153 to unearth some very interest numerical relationships encoded within.

$$\boxed{153 \mid 351}$$

The mirror of **153** is **351**, which is nothing more than the sum of the numbers 1 - 26 added together:

$1 + 2 + 3 + 4 + 5 + 6 + 7 + 8 + $ $9 + 10 + 11 + 12 + 13 + 14 + 15 + 16 + 17 + 18 + 19 + 20 + 21 + 22 + 23 + 24 + 25 + \underline{26} = 351$

The number **351** thus refers not only to the 26 letters of our alphabet, the numerical sum of *LordGod*, the Hebraic Tetragrammaton, but also to the center of our galaxy denoted by the numerical equivalents of *Scorpio, black hole, center*, and *mother*. *Write* and *Scribe* both equal 26 as well and what else do we *Write /Scribe* but the 26 letters of our alphabet?!

Adding the mirrors of **153** and **351** yields the most interesting number of **504**. (153 + 351 = **504**). This multiplied by 10 yields us the combined radii of the Earth and Moon being **5,040** miles, or the number we get when we square the circle of the Earth.

The divisors of 153 are 1, 3, 9, 17, 51, and 153. Added together these six numbers sum to **234** (1 + 3 + 9 + 17 + 51 + 153 = **234**). We saw that in our chapter on the Solar System that the numerical equivalents of our 9 planets and Sun summed to **234** (shown again below).

☉ ☿ ♀ ⊕ ♂ ♃ ♄ ⛢ ♆ ♇
13 + 27 + 23 + 24 + 13 + 35 + 26 + 25 + 28 + 20 = 234

We also know that adding the mirror of 234, or 432, together sums to that beastly number **666** (234 + 432 = **666**). We can also find the number **666** within the number 153. Adding the numbers 1 through 17 will sum to 153. (1 + 2 + 3 + 4 + 5 ......16 + 17 = **153**). If we pull out the prime numbers within these first 17 digits, with *17 being the seventh prime number*, square these numbers, and add them together, lo and behold it will sum to St. John's number of wisdom, or **666**.

$$2^2 \quad 3^2 \quad 5^2 \quad 7^2 \quad 11^2 \quad 13^2 \quad 17^2$$
$$4 + 9 + 25 + 49 + 121 + 169 + 289 = 666$$

The number 153 can also lead us back to the high civilization of the Greeks. Many of the stories within the Bible were said to have been borrowed or adapted from ancient Greek mythologies and many believe the entire Bible itself is actually an amalgamation of Hindu, Greek, Egyptian, Zoroastrian, and Pagan myths. The Greeks had two terms for God; Thea and Theos. Thea was the female term for God and Theos was the male term and it is most likely where we derive the word *The*. Etymologically speaking, it is most interesting that every time you speak the word *The* you are actually referring to divinity. If we take the English word *The* and place a decimal place between the 6 and 5, and give it a female and male distinction, adding these together will once again yield us the number **153** (76.5 + 76.5 = **153**).

$$\text{THE} \quad \text{THE}$$
$$7\,6.5 \; + \; 7\,6.5 = \mathbf{153}$$

This male and female God, denoted by *The*, or *Theos* and *Thea* and the number 153, can also be found within the womb of all creation, or the Vesica Piscis. Piscis refers to the constellation Pisces which is symbolized as two fish. The fishes caught in the story are most certainly a reference to this fundamental geometric symbol. Jesus being a "fisher of men" is yet again pointing to the symbol of our universal birth. Using the adage of "As above, so below", we can find a fish swimming down towards Earth and a fish swimming up towards the heavens - representing both the male and female. We saw in Volume 1 that *fish* equals 23 equating to *circle, heaven, temple,* and *beauty.* In early Christianity, it was said that the man would draw one side of the fish and the female the other, symbolically referencing not only Christ, but the duality within creation.

Female   Male

If make the width of a Vesica Piscis equal to 1, then its height would be exactly equal to the square root of 3. If we make the width of the fish equal to **153**, then the height would be 265. 265/153 is an excellent approximation of the square root of our holy number 3.

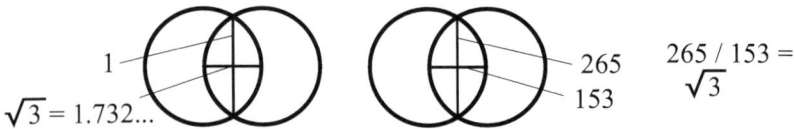

$$1 \qquad \sqrt{3} = 1.732... \qquad 265 \qquad 153 \qquad 265 \,/\, 153 = \sqrt{3}$$

The Freemasons often referred to God as a *Grand Architect,* and we know of Jesus as being a carpenter. Common sense tells us that due to God's title and Jesus's occupation that they both must have had an intimate knowledge of mathematics and geometry. Jesus being symbolized as a fish is yet again evidence that he was well versed with the numerical properties of symbols, such as the Vesica Piscis. Trigonometry is the study of triangles and the relationships between their sides and the angles between these sides. Since the trinity, or triangle, is one of the most important geometric forms in all creation, there should be no surprise that we find some important numerology with the core functions of trigonometry. Trigonometry has six main functions called *Sine, Cosine, Tangent, Cotangent, Secant,* and *Cosecant.* If we define a triangle with sides of length **a, b, c** and the angle θ, we can define our six trigonometric functions as follows:

$$\sin \theta = \frac{b}{c} \quad \cos \theta = \frac{a}{c} \quad \tan \theta = \frac{b}{a}$$

$$\csc \theta = \frac{c}{b} \quad \sec \theta = \frac{a}{b} \quad \cot \theta = \frac{a}{b}$$

$$a = \cos \theta \text{ and } b = \sin \theta$$

$$\underbrace{a^2 + b^2 = c^2}$$

$$\cos^2 \theta + \sin^2 \theta = 1$$

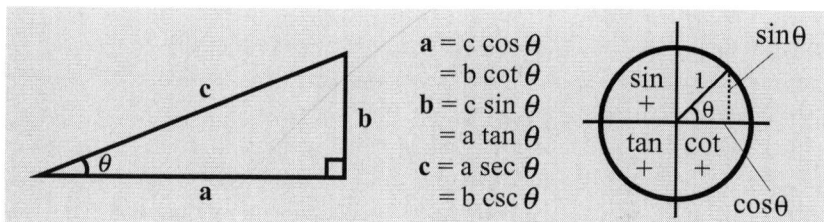

$$a = c \cos \theta$$
$$= b \cot \theta$$
$$b = c \sin \theta$$
$$= a \tan \theta$$
$$c = a \sec \theta$$
$$= b \csc \theta$$

Using our cipher, the numerical equivalents of these six functions when added together sum to none other than **153** (17 + 22 + 29 + 34 + 23 + 28 = **153**).

SINE
6 5 1 5 = **17**

COSINE
3 2 6 5 1 5 = **22**

TANGENT
7 1 1 7 5 1 7 = **29**

COTANGENT
3 2 7 1 1 7 5 1 7 = **34**

SECANT
6 5 3 1 1 7 = **23**

COSECANT
3 2 6 5 3 1 1 7 = **28**

153

Even the number of days in the solar year (**365.24**), as well as the number of feet in an English mile, **5,280**, sums to this magical number!

THREE HUNDRED SIXTY FIVE POINT TWO FOUR = **153**
7 6 5 5 5   6 6 1 4 5 5 4   6 5 3 7 2   6 5 5 5   3 2 5 1 7   7 4   2 6 2 6 5

FIVE THOUSAND TWO HUNDRED EIGHTY FEET = **153**
6 5 5 5   7 6 2 6 6 1 1 4   7 4 2   6 6 1 4 5 5 4   5 5 7 6 7 2 6 5 5 7

God is some mathematician!

As we saw earlier in the chapter, on our Sun God Horus as well as in Volume 1 of this text, the square root of the number **153** can be found in the perfect 5, 12, 13 Pythagorean triangle. When we separate the adjacent side of the triangle into 2 and 3, we find the length of the line to be **12.369**, which is the square root of **153** (shown again below). By multiplying this by a lunar month of 29.53 days, we find an almost perfect correlation between the lunar and solar year with the solar year being **365.24** days. (12.369 x 29.53 days = 365.25).

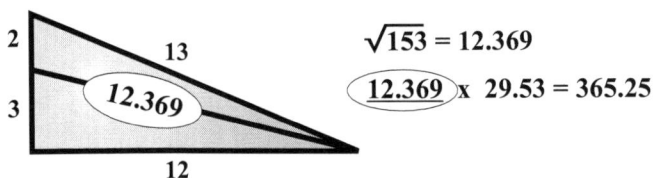

$$\sqrt{153} = 12.369$$

$$12.369 \times 29.53 = 365.25$$

The last thing we can learn from the number **153** is its relationship to the *Ark* in scripture. We all know of the Ark of the Covenant, a mythological container or chest that held the Ten Commandments written in stone by Moses, as well as the *Ark* Noah built and sailed on, carrying the next generation of species of man and animal to dry land after the deluge. Using homonyms as our guide, it should be easily recognizable that *Ark* is most definitely a reference to the mathematical *Arc*. Both **C** and **K** in our cipher are delineated by the number 3 and henceforth both the *Ark* and *Arc* give us the numbers, read left to right, **1, 5** and **3**. Viewing this numerologically, we can see that the *Ark/Arc* gives us the number **153**.

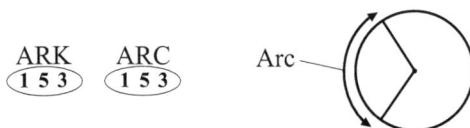

ARK   ARC   Arc
1 5 3   1 5 3

An ark is nothing more than a ship, and yet again we see a reference to this number symbolism in the story of Jesus' miraculous catch of fish. The layer upon layer of mathematical symbolism is pure genius, and stories like this are begging its readers to look deep within the text to unearth the magic that lie therein. Could the radii of the Earth and Moon, the numerology of our Solar System, the six trigonometric functions, the days of the solar year, the number of feet in a mile, the geometry of the Vesica Piscis, the beastly number 666, the math to map our sun and moon and the *ark* in scripture really be encoded within this miraculous number? Cast your net to *the right side and ye shall find*.

THE 3.5 OF PI

According to Hinduism, the universe started with an *all-encompassing* (or *One*) vibratory word or essence called *AUM* (Though it is sometimes spelled "Om" - summing to **3**). The three syllables that make up this mighty sound, as we have seen, are symbolized by a **3** and a tail swirling out its back. We correlated this great vibratory *AUM* to *Pi* in the first Volume and interestingly *AUM*, *Pi* and *One* all sum to **8**.

$$\text{ॐ} \qquad \underset{1\ 6\ 1\ =\ \mathbf{8}}{\text{AUM}} \qquad \underset{3\ 5\ =\ \mathbf{8}}{\text{PI}} \qquad \underset{2\ 1\ 5\ =\ \mathbf{8}}{\text{ONE}}$$

So many spiritual practices of the past claim that the human being is microcosm of the macrocosm, an idea we have explored in depth in both Volumes of this text. Hinduism believes that within the universe of man exists an all powerful, serpentine force lying dormant named Kundalini which means "coiled power" or "she who is ring-shaped" residing in the sacrum at the base of the spine. Through meditation, contemplation, passion, study, commitment, and various other spiritual exercises, this serpent may be raised up through the seven chakras, or wheels, and through what are known as the three gunas that are present within the subtle body. These chakras are energetic points active in the endocrine system of glands, each of which secretes different types of hormones directly into the blood stream. Once all 7 chakras are illuminated, a profound transformation takes place within the individual. This transformation has been called an awakening or enlightenment and is the physical and spiritual transformation lying behind every religion. Matthew 10:16 informs us to "be as wise as serpents" and is a direct reference to this ancient Hindu divinatory practice. Most important to our study though are the numerical principles surrounding this energetic serpent. The Kundalini is said to rise up one's spine *3 and a half times*. Each coil is said to represent one of the three gunas (Tamas, Rajas, Sattva) with the half coil signifying *transcendence*. In modern quantum theory, quantum particles, the fundamental particles said to compose matter, have a variance of spin being 0 spin, ½ spin, 1 spin, and 2 spin, making for a total of *3 and a half spin*. It is indeed most interesting that modern science and ancient wisdom seem to coincide perfectly when speaking of the spinning, coiled fundamental energy within all matter. Placing a decimal place between the 3 and 5 in Pi yields us *this 3 and a half.*

$$\underset{3.5}{\text{P I}}$$

Once the Kundalini serpent rises up to the 7th chakra and into the pineal gland, or the "seat of the soul," the initiate undergoes a profound realization on the nature of reality and his place in it. This mental and physical evolutionary process of awakening is the organic religion existing within all things. It is the inherent process of all things coming to fruition. The human being experiences this awakening as the full realization that he or she is an aspect of the living God and is therefore the creator gazing at his creation through the human vessel. At her height, the Kundalini serpent simply wishes to remind us of the power of our temple and the infinite love the creator has for its creation. The Kundalini serpent may make her travels up our spine and into our heads, but she still wishes to tell us of *the power of our two hands.*

KUNDALINI
3 6 1 4 1 2 5 1 5 = **28**

The process of Kundalini according to Swami Rama, the three gunas, seven chakras and their physical (earthly)/cosmic (heavenly) distinctions, are listed below. As we discussed earlier, the process of Kundalini is easily recognized in the 33 degrees of Scottish Rite Freemasonry, with the 33 bones of one's spine being the degrees or levels the spinal fluid, or chrism must climb to reach the pineal gland.

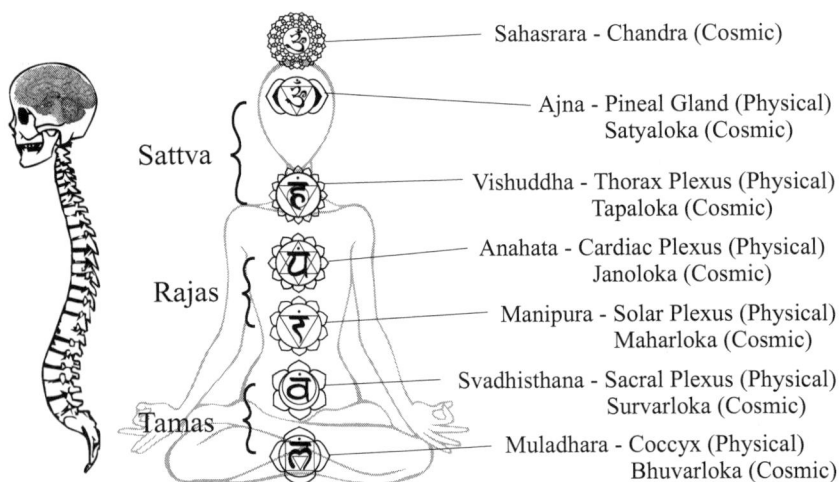

Sattva
Rajas
Tamas

Sahasrara - Chandra (Cosmic)

Ajna - Pineal Gland (Physical)
Satyaloka (Cosmic)

Vishuddha - Thorax Plexus (Physical)
Tapaloka (Cosmic)

Anahata - Cardiac Plexus (Physical)
Janoloka (Cosmic)

Manipura - Solar Plexus (Physical)
Maharloka (Cosmic)

Svadhisthana - Sacral Plexus (Physical)
Survarloka (Cosmic)

Muladhara - Coccyx (Physical)
Bhuvarloka (Cosmic)

The Hindi yogi Swami Vivekananda described kundalini briefly in London during his lectures on Raja Yoga:

According to the Yogis, there are two nerve currents in the spinal column, called Pingalâ and Idâ, and a hollow canal called Sushumnâ running through the spinal cord. At the lower end of the hollow canal is what the Yogis call the "Lotus of the Kundalini". They describe it as triangular in form in which, in the symbolical language of the Yogis, there is a power called the Kundalini, coiled up. When that Kundalini awakes, it tries to force a passage through this hollow canal, and as it rises step by step, as it were, layer after layer of the mind becomes open and all the different visions and wonderful powers come to the Yogi. If we take the figure eight horizontally ∞ there are two parts which are connected in the middle. Suppose you add eight after eight, piled one on top of the other, that will represent the spinal cord. The left is the Ida, the right Pingala, and that hollow canal which runs through the centre of the spinal cord is the Sushumna.

The *Numerology* of the hollow canal, or *Sushumna* that the Kundalini serpent rises up, finds us the **33** bones in our *Spinal Column*.

NUMEROLOGY
1 6 1 5 5 2 2 2 7 2 = 33

SUSHUMNA
6 6 6 6 6 1 1 1 = 33

SPINAL COLUMN
6 3 5 1 1 2 3 2 2 6 1 1 = 33

According to Swami Vivekananda, the ascending energy of the Kundalini serpent rises up the spine through essentially stacked eights. The 3 and a half turns of Pi, and Pi also summing to 8, give us the precise two mathematical serpentine paths attributed to this ancient spiritual practice. The quest for enlightenment seems to be inextricably linked to Pi. We can find confirmation of this in the Tarot deck.

STRENGTH.

Our 3.5 of Pi sums to **8**. The 8th card of the Tarot deck is *Strength*.

STRENGTH
6 7 5 5 1 7 7 6 = **44**

Notice the infinite **8** above the head of the 8th card of the tarot deck. There are 22 cards in the deck which means *Strength* would be 14th card from the last (**44/14** = Pi).

114

The 3.5 of Pi can also be found in Egypt. Both Pi and Phi, as we have previously seen, can be found in the Great Pyramid of Giza shown again below.

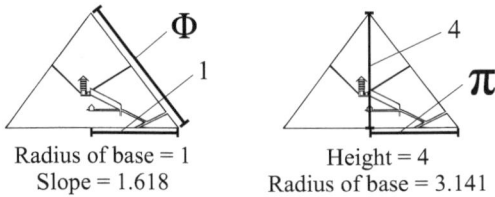

Radius of base = 1
Slope = 1.618

Height = 4
Radius of base = 3.141

Notice the difference between Pi and Phi is merely the letter **H**. Using the Egyptian alphabet, we can find a congruence with the letter **H** and some of the sacred mathematical principles of nature. The letter **H** in the Egyptian alphabet has two distinctions as shown below. One of the letters is a twisted cord or rope that is turned 3 and a half times and the other H is a coil, unfurling out from its center. Could this **H** and the difference between the **H** in Pi and Phi be references to these fundamental mathematical ratios? It does not take much imagination to see the unfurling sequence of the Fibonacci numbers in the symbol of one of the Hs, and the 3.5 of our Pi seems to speak to this letter as well.

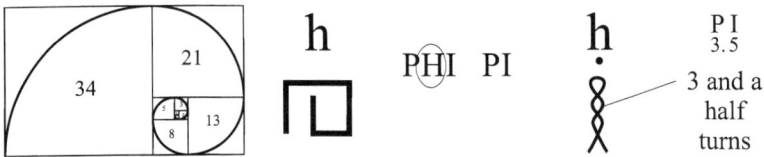

There can be no doubt that the Egyptian's entire culture was based around sacred number, sacred geometry, and symbol. The Egyptians basked in the glory of their understanding of God and the natural world. The quest for enlightenment was the only quest worth undertaking, according to the Egyptians, for this was man's sole purpose for being on Earth - to recognize his own divine nature and lift himself up from the lower animal kingdom. Every temple, statue, and piece of art crafted in Egypt spoke of the glory of the kingdom of God. The serpent seen protruding from the "third eye" in so many Egyptian statues is archeological evidence that this alchemical, Hindu, and Freemasonic spiritual ascent was well-known by the Egyptians. Many believe Africa, and specifically Egypt, was the birthplace of not only man, but also of this ancient divinatory practice. By understanding mathematics, the language of God, and Pi, the most powerful ratio in all of mathematics, the Egyptians came to know the most intimate part of themselves - *the God within.*

GENESIS 1:1

The Christian Kabbalist Carlo Suares, writing of the Hebrew Bible, said, *"In the severity of its beginning, in its first chapter, in its first verse, in its first sequence of letter-numbers, is the seed and in the seed is the whole."* This exact sentiment is expressed in Genesis 1:29, "And God said Behold, I have given you every herb bearing seed, which is upon the face of all the earth, and every tree, in which is the fruit of a tree yielding seed." This fundamental idea expressed within the first page of Genesis is important to understand, for it introduces us to one of the most integral and essential philosophies that exists throughout nature: *self-reference.* Self-referentialism is nature's calling card, for nature needs nothing but the essence of herself to continue her own evolution. In mathematics this self-reference is seen in the Fibonacci sequence, something we explored in depth in Volume 1. The Fibonacci Sequence starts with 0 and 1, or what we identified as our "Holy" and "Spirit," and it needs nothing more than these first two numbers to flourish, unfold and complexify its beauty in numinous ways. We also see this self-referentialism in the mathematics of fractals. Fractals are a mathematical phenomenon rediscovered by Benoit Mendelbroit and, in short, express self-similarity across scales. Or, in other words, the part looks like the whole and the whole looks like the part. Much like the seed of a tree, the entire essence of the tree exists within the seed and the seed was born from the original tree, and the original tree was born from a seed, etc. Without self-reference, all of nature would cease to exist, and Genesis wished to inform us of this absolute truth in the poetic fashion in which it was written.

The first verse of Genesis serves as a primer for understanding the rest of the text. A *primer* is defined as "an elementary text for teaching children to read." Understanding the symbolic, mathematical, and spiritual essence of the first verse, allows one access into the deeper insights that lay hidden within the myriad verses and stories contained within the rest of the text. It is the seed, or verse, that contains within it the whole tree or essence of the entire book. Just like when painting a wall in your house, if the *primer* isn't laid first, the outer layers of paint will not stick. Without planting the first verse, or seed, within the grounds of your own understanding, the tree that is the Holy Bible can cannot grow and branch out its wisdom into your life. Intuiting this fundamental philosophy allows us direct access into the occult, or hidden beauty, within the Holy Bible.

Before we launch into the first verse of Genesis itself, let us first look into the title of this first verse, or Genesis 1:1. Using just a bit of creativity, *the alchemists finest tool*, we can see that before Genesis tells us anything about heaven and earth or the glory of God's creation, it wishes to tell us about Pi. Using our cipher, Genesis sums to **35**. If we remove the colon between the 1 and 1 in Genesis 1:1, and we place a decimal point between the 3 and 5 in the sum of Genesis, this leaves us with two numbers, 11 and 3.5. 11 divided by 3.5 is none other than 3.142, or Pi.

$$\text{GENESIS } \underset{7\;5\;1\;5\;6\;5\;6\;=\;35}{\text{1:1}} \begin{array}{l} \rule{1cm}{0.4pt}\;\mathbf{11} \\ \rule{1cm}{0.4pt}\;\mathbf{3.5} \end{array} \Big\}\; \mathbf{11\,/\,3.5 = 3.142\;\pi}$$

And let us not forget, the three numbers between the 12 of *Holy* and 16 of *Bible* are **13**, **14**, and **15**, three numbers we've come to know so well. The fact the Genesis encodes Pi in such creative ways speaks volumes on the nature of our creator and the nature of the essence of its being. The Vesica Piscis is considered the womb of all creation (and references our supernal cosmic mother *Isis*, with *Genesis* being indeed the *genes of Isis*). Before there could be a womb, or two circles that overlap each other, we must assume that symbolically the first form in existence must have been simply one circle, denoted by our sacred geometrical 3 of heaven. The circle marks a distinction between the inner and the outer and, as we know, it geometrically encapsulates the most amount of space in 2 dimensions. Since dimension, geometry, and matter itself had not yet been created, and were merely archetypal potentials existing within the mind of God, this beginning can only be spoken of as pure metaphor (and what we can identify as *No Thing*). But it is a mathematical metaphor that can lead us to a fundamental understanding of how the Grand Architect worked his magic in creating our universe. This circle, or mind of God, can be viewed as the primordial egg we spoke of in Volume 1. The potential of all of our manifested reality existed within this egg, or circle of creation, and as we are told through nursery rhyme and mythology, one day this egg cracked. Humpty Dumpty took a fall and God said, "Let there be light!" To signify this cracking, we can draw a line straight down the middle of this first heavenly circle in existence, creating the diameter we need to find its circumference. It was in this moment that Pi was formed, and its infinite digits went unfurling out, creating our universe.

Sacred Geometrical Heaven (The *No Thing*)   **3** | π 3.14159.... *The Cracking of Pi*

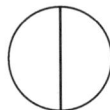

This initial *cracking of Pi,* or severing of the first circle in existence, resulted in the differentiation of light and the division of God's essence into manifestation. With this divine light came the geometry, form and substance of all that is. It also created two halves analogous to the polar opposites existing throughout the world; the left and right hemispheres of your brain, Adam and Eve, day and night, good and evil, etc. This scission, or cutting open, creating the womb of creation is recognized in the Vesica **Pi**scis, or better stated as the *Vessel of the Pi Scission.* Most important to note, though there was a division in our first moments of creation, this division was not completed divided, for if it were the entire universe would have fallen apart long ago. We see this division and paradoxical connectedness in the womb of the Vesica Piscis. The overlapping circles are divided from one another, yet they remained unified. *They are separate but one.* These two circles represent a 2 dimensional symbolic representation of the *halving of our Pi.* This symbol, with its two circles and nested womb between them create a total of three geometric forms, recognized by our Holy Trinity. It also leads us to the famous alchemical Axiom of Maria that states, "The one becomes the two, the two becomes the three and out of the third comes the one as the fourth." This *One as the Fourth* in the axiom, we can see as symbolically representing the earthly square of 4, as well as the first *squared circle representing the merging of both heaven and earth into one.*

"The one"   "becomes the two,"   "the two becomes the three"

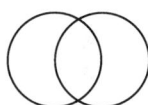

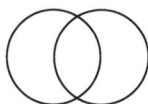

"and out of the third"   "comes the *one* as the fourth."

This unification of heaven and earth becoming one is philosophically stated in the phrase "As above, so below" and confirmed to us in Genesis 1:1, telling us that both Heaven and Earth were created by God *simultaneously*: "In the beginning God created *the Heaven and the Earth.*" Since we have explored the geometry of our first moments of creation, let us now turn our focus to the letters and numbers encoded within the first verse of Genesis and to the seed which containeth the whole tree.

The numerical equivalent of Genesis 1:1 sums to **190**.

IN THE BEGINNING GOD CREATED THE HEAVEN AND THE EARTH.
51 765 25 751151 7 724 3551754 765 651551 114 765 51576

(**190**)

We will explore this number in depth in the following pages but first, since we know Genesis 1:1 seems to want to inform us about that infinite transcendental number of Pi, let us first see if there is any connection between the two. Genesis 1:1 is composed of ten words, referencing not only our base ten system, our ten fingers, as well as the Pythagorean Tetractys, but as well will see, the first ten digits of Pi as well. Using our cipher, we can assign the numerical equivalents to the first ten digits of Pi, **3.141592653**, and the very words we use to speak these digits, or *Three Point One Four One Five Nine Two Six Five Three*. Assigning the numerical equivalents to these words, a truly remarkable correspondence occurs, for when we add the sum total of these eleven words (*including Point*), it sums to **190** as well.

3.141592653

THREE POINT ONE FOUR ONE FIVE NINE TWO SIX FIVE THREE
76555 32517 2156265 2156555 1515 742 653 6555 76555

(**190**)

Interestingly if we add these first ten digits of Pi together, it sums to **39**, the numerical equivalent of *Christian, Sine/Cosine, Stargate, Golden Rule, Great Work* and *Freemasonry* ($3 + 1 + 4 + 1 + 5 + 9 + 2 + 6 + 5 + 3 = 39$). It would seem that numerically, Freemasonry, the Great Work, and being a Christian seem to be inextricably linked to Pi. These ten digits equaling **39** is also a direct reference to the Old Testament as well, for it is composed of **39** books. Multiplying these ten digits results in the number 97,200 ($3 \times 1 \times 4 \times 1 \times 5 \times 9 \times 2 \times 6 \times 5 \times 3 = 97,200$). If we divide this by the 360 degrees of a circle, we yield the number **270** ($97,200 / 360 = 270$). **270** is the Hebraic numerical equivalent of **INRI** (**I** - Yod 10, **N** - Nun 50, **R** - Resh 200, **1** - Yod 10, equaling **270**), the words above Jesus upon his crucifixion. **270** is 9 months and **39** is the roughly the number of weeks in 9 months. 9 months is amount of time in human gestation. Could it be that the birth of creation is directly related to the numbers associated with the birth of human beings? According to the math, it would seem so.

119

Could the Bible have been written *mathematically first,* and the stories only then laid over this fundamental mathematical foundation? If so, was the ratio of Pi the foundation upon which they worked? There is a legend that the Torah, or first five books of the Old Testament, was written two thousand years before the creation of the world. According to many scholars, it was written with no spaces between the letters to allow for numerous translations when reading. We just explored the idea that the first form before creation was the circle and that circle became our mighty, holy ratio of Pi upon its split. If the Bible was indeed based on such a fundamental mathematical constant such as Pi, then the symbolic legend of the Torah, being written *before creation*, ceases to be so outlandish.

Genesis 1:1 and the numerology of **3.141592653**, both summing to **190**, point us to yet another quite astounding numerical correspondence. The Greek philosopher Plato identified 5 geometric forms, now known as the Platonic Solids, that could fit perfectly inside a sphere. These five forms have been known since antiquity and have found their place, time and time again, within the pages of astrological, esoteric, alchemical and Hermetic studies. In Volume 1 we saw how these 5 forms could fit within the Holy 108 of the Fibonacci Sequence and its geometric equivalent known as Metatron's Cube (see Vol. 1 p. 76). These five solids are the Tetrahedron, Hexahedron, Octahedron, Icosahedron, and Dodecahedron and are illustrated below. If we add up the faces, edges, and sides of all five of these solids, it sums to, once again, **190**.

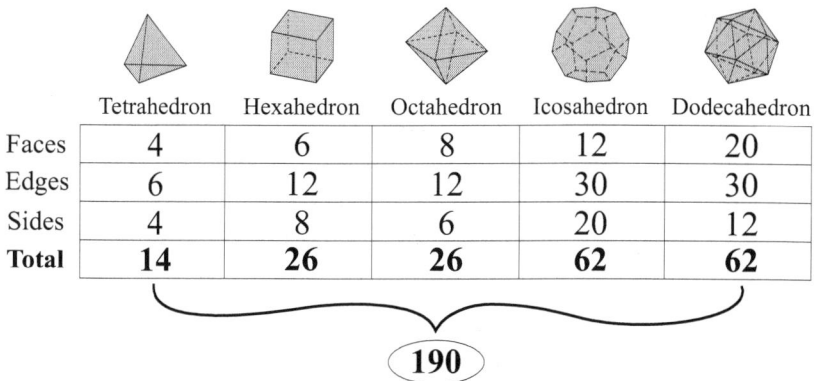

	Tetrahedron	Hexahedron	Octahedron	Icosahedron	Dodecahedron
Faces	4	6	8	12	20
Edges	6	12	12	30	30
Sides	4	8	6	20	12
Total	**14**	**26**	**26**	**62**	**62**

190

It is quite remarkable, and surely not a coincidence, that these numerical correspondences are found within the first verse. But the authors of the Bible had much more in store for us as we will see.

We have explored in depth the power of the symbol known as the Greek Monad or Egyptian Sun glyph. This symbol, like the Star of David comes with the adage of "As above, so below," the central point being the Lord, the *So below*, or Singularity within the *As above*, or Wholeness of God's creation. This simple symbol speaks of a fundamental scientific philosophy within our universe, and that is of the inherent division yet oneness of all things. This philosophy and symbol points to the fact that Man and God are equals, and the singular point of consciousness that we call "I" is nothing more and nothing less than God viewing his creation *through you*.

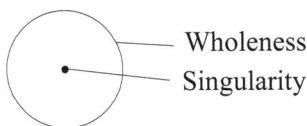

— Wholeness
— Singularity

The Greeks gave this symbol the numerical value of **361** and what we came to understand in Volume 1 as the 360 degrees of a circle encapsulating the entirety of creation and the "One" *being you*. In our studies on the English Alphabet, we assigned the numbers to the letters of our alphabet using a septenary system, or base seven system. Though we have decoded Genesis 1:1 with this system, the number of words in this first verse, or ten, wishes to stress the importance of our base ten system. Have we found ourselves at a crossroads?

We can convert a number from a base ten system to a base seven system with relative ease. When we do this with the numerical equivalent of Genesis 1:1 and the first ten digits of Pi, equaling **190**, we can find yet another astounding numerical correspondence. **190** in a base seven system equals **361**! The creation of heaven and earth in Genesis would therefore seem to point directly to not only a symbol and philosophy shared by the Greeks and Egyptians, but also to your role and place in the cosmic drama that is this existence. Converting a number from base ten to base seven is shown below. By finding the whole numbers that divide closely into each division of 7, we can carry out the remaining number and find our conversion.

190 / 7 (27 x 7 = <u>189</u>) - remaining **1**
<u>27</u> / 7 (3 x 7 = <u>21</u>) - remaining **6**
21 / 7 = 3 - remaining **3**

361 = Greek Monad
(360° and *you*)

The square root of **361** is **19** (19 x 19 = **361**). If we climb up the number ladder from 0 - 19 and add the digits as we ascend, it will sum to **190,** giving us yet another reference to the Greek Monad and Egyptian Sun symbol (0 + 1 + 2 + 3 + 4 + 5 + 6 + 7 + 8 + 9 + 10 + 11 + 12 + 13 + 14 + 15 + 16 + 17 + 18 + 19 = **190**). These first twenty digits (*counting zero as a digit*) become a direct reference to your 10 fingers and 10 toes, or the complete man - whole, holy, crafted by the hands of God and made from his image. These 20 numbers also establish some of the most fundamental mathematical ratios and concepts within creation. 0-9 is our base ten system, 10, 11, and 12 sum to the supremely esoteric *thirty-three*, 13, 14 and 15 establish Pi (3.1415), 16 and 18 give us the ratio of Phi (1.618), the 17 barring 16 and 18 from joining reference the magical number 153 (adding 1-17 sums to 153), and 19 is the square root of the Greek Monad and the number encoded in the primer, or first verse of Genesis. All of this illustrated easily by walking up our number line.

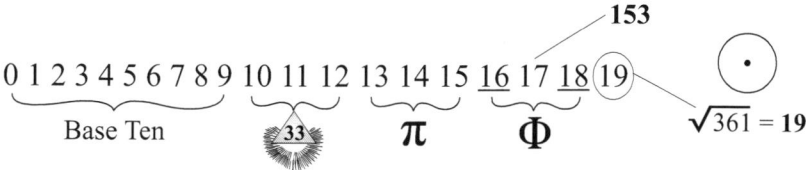

The creation of our number line is the unfolding story of the mathematics of our universe, laid out for us in the simplest of manner. The creation of heaven and earth in Genesis 1:1, pointing to the number **190**, if viewed in a creative way, sets a foundation for understanding some of the most important mathematical principles created by God.

Using our cipher, we can find this magical number **190** in yet another interesting way within the first verse of Genesis, and that is relating it directly to the English Alphabet. Let's concentrate on the individual letters within the first verse of Genesis and cross off the letters not used in our alphabet. For instance, since the letters **X** or **Z** are not used, we will cross them out. Since **C** and **D** are used, we will leave them.

IN THE BEGINNING GOD CREATED THE HEAVEN AND THE EARTH.

A B C D E X̶ G H I X̶ X̶ X̶ M̶ N O X̶ X̶ R X̶ T X̶ V X̶ X̶ X̶ X̶

In doing so, this leaves 12 letters: **A, B, C, D, E, G, H, I, N, O, R, T,** and **V**. Once again, *Twelve* in our cipher sums to 28, representing your hands as well as being the numerical equivalent of *Holy Bible*.

Using our cipher, let's now assign the numerical equivalents for each of the letters we have left.

A B C D E ⅀ G H I ⅀ ⅀ ⅀ ⅀ N O ⅀ ⅀ R ⅀ T ⅀ V ⅀ ⅀ ⅀ ⅀
1 2 3 4 5   7 6 5   1 2   5   7   5

The next thing we can do is find out how many times each of the letters are used in the verse and multiply this by their numerical equivalent. For instance, the letter **A** is used 4 times, once in each of the words *created*, *Heaven*, *and*, and *Earth*. Since **A** has the value of 1 and we are using it four times, we can now assign the letter **A** the value of **4**. Since the letter **B** is only used once in the verse, in the word **Beginning** and has the value of **2**, we will leave this letter with the value of **2**. The new values for each of the letters are shown below.

A B C D E ⅀ G H I ⅀ ⅀ ⅀ ⅀ N O ⅀ ⅀ R ⅀ T ⅀ V ⅀ ⅀ ⅀ ⅀
4 2 3 12 45   21 30 15   6 2   10   35   5

If we add up the new values for each of the letters, lo and behold we find that magical number **190** once again $(4 + 2 + 3 + 12 + 45 + 21 + 30 + 15 + 6 + 2 + 10 + 35 + 5 = 190)$!

Such a construction is truly astounding and points directly to the gnostic revelatory manner in which the Bible was written. Writers who had a direct relationship to deity, leaving their wisdom for you and I to rediscover.

One more interesting thing we will see with our holy number **190** is once again found in the digits of Pi. Notice a balancing point can be established in the first ten digits of Pi on the number **59**, with four digits to the left and four to the right. We saw the power of this number in the first text with *Jesus Christ, Alchemical Wedding, Alchemical Marriage, Knight's Templar, In God We Trust, Reborn Christian*, and *English Alphabet* all summing to **59**. Interesting to note, these first ten digits also begin and end with a **3**, referencing the number **33** once again.

3.141**59**2653

This number **59** will lead us into the next chapter and to one of the most important things that God created, and that is the pump organ within the church of you, *your very own heart.*

WEIGHING THE HEART

In Volume 1 we looked at the cosmological makeup of man, where the 12 constellations of the Zodiac are placed onto the body of a human being. This idea expressed by our ancestors was well known by many cultures and solidified the fundamental philosophy declared by Hermes, "*As above, so below.*" The stars above reflect the light of spirit within you. The Milky Way is but a banner or body of stars reflecting the temple of the human being: Aries was assigned to the head, Taurus was the neck, etc. This anatomical and physiological zodiacal makeup is shown once again below.

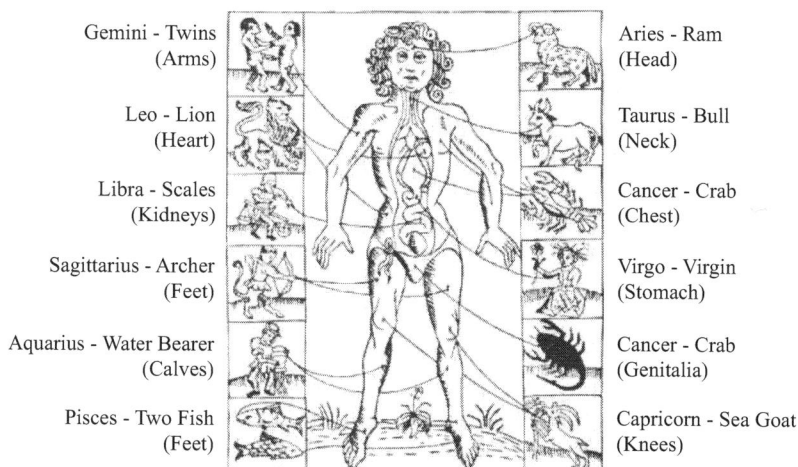

Gemini - Twins (Arms)		Aries - Ram (Head)
Leo - Lion (Heart)		Taurus - Bull (Neck)
Libra - Scales (Kidneys)		Cancer - Crab (Chest)
Sagittarius - Archer (Feet)		Virgo - Virgin (Stomach)
Aquarius - Water Bearer (Calves)		Cancer - Crab (Genitalia)
Pisces - Two Fish (Feet)		Capricorn - Sea Goat (Knees)

In this chapter we will be focusing on the Lion, or Leo, the constellation assigned to the *Heart* of our cosmological man. The lion has most often been symbolic of strength, nobility, courage, and determination. A warrior being *lionhearted* is a direct reference to his or her passion and leadership. The heart is the organ that pumps our blood, the color of blood being red which has always been a color associated with passion. This passion is attributed to the passion and zest for life - a passion driven by honesty, love, commitment, and understanding. It is having the bravery, strength, and gusto to walk one's own path with the yearning to find the truth of the light of the spirit within. This spiritual light has often been also associated with the color gold, signifying the light of the sun and the alchemical gold within the lead of one's lower animal nature. The lion is golden in color, and his fierceness and position as ruler of the animal kingdom is symbolic of one's own journey through the material world. One must become a lion and tame his animal nature to reach the glory of the kingdom of God above.

The lower animal nature of the human being is denoted by the three lower chakras, something we explored in the chapter the "3.5 of Pi". Making the ascension through these lower wheels and into the realms of the heart chakra is part of the spiritual quest we all must take to find the god who dwells within. The spiritual quest, the alchemical process, and the rebirth of the Christian is individualized for each person and *no one*, not guru, zen master, or minister can tell you the path you must take. They may present to you clues, philosophies, and wisdom, but in the end, the search for one's spirit must be done by you and you alone. No one but you can find the path to your higher spiritual self.

The lower animal nature is shed at the gateway to the heart. The animal aspect of our nature only resides here on Earth - for the heavens is the territory where pure spirit dwells and no animal essence may pass into these higher domains. It is no coincidence that *Earth* is merely an anagram for *Heart*. This gate, from the lower realms of the atavistic to the upper realms of the spirit, is where the earthly being is shed and the newly awakened spiritual being is born. This gateway to the higher spiritual self was known and symbolized in so many cultures as the Lion's Gate. A few very notable examples are the Babylonian gates of Ishtar, the Sphinx of Egypt, and the Imperial Gardens in the Forbidden City of China. The Sumerian mother goddess of fertility, Inanna is shown below standing on two symmetrical lions. In each of her hands she is holding what appears to be a *zero* and a *line* - could this possibly be a reference to what we symbolically named the *Holy* and *Spirit*? Notice she is naked (which is a symbolic reference to her being of spirit and without *earthly matter*). She has wings ascending her to the highest heights and is flanked by two owls, which have been forever known as symbols of wisdom (quite possibly because of their ability to see quite nearly 360 degrees).

Following one's heart allows one to make the decisions that will ultimately lead him or her to a glorified life. Allowing oneself to flow like water, take things as they come, appreciate what one has, and never asking for more than one needs are the ways of the heart. The heart yearns for nothing more than love and communion with nature and all of her beautiful creations. The mystics of the past understood that nature will provide amply to those who appreciate all she has to offer. Those who are never satisfied with their material wealth, or only wish for notoriety and personal glory, will never find the path to the Lion's Gate. The Lion's Gate exists only for those who are strong enough, brave enough, and *passionate* enough to search for the golden, gleaming spirit within. The Lion's Gate resides in us all, but the entrance can only be found if one follows one's heart.

The heart was known by the Egyptians to be *the most important* organ within the temple of man. The crux of Egyptian philosophy was in fact based entirely around this organ. In the Egyptian Book of the Dead, there is a ceremony known as *The Weighing of the Heart Ceremony* and was the ceremony that was performed upon one's death. The idea was that one's heart would be weighed against the feather of Ma'at. If it weighed less than a feather, the initiate would be allowed into the gates of heaven. The scene as it is sketched in the Book of the Dead is shown below.

The metaphor of one's heart weighing less than a feather is a direct reference to one living a life of passion. Being *heartfelt* is recognizing the world and one's life as sacred, never giving in to the difficult challenges one faces whilst undertaking the journey of life, having deep respect and admiration for your fellow human being, loving in earnest, and being true to thyself. The elevation of one's heart with the purest of love is the philosophy the Egyptians followed and so adored and is a philosophy that is, without a doubt, absolutely pertinent to humans today.

The numerical equivalent of *The Weighing of the Heart Ceremony* sums to **132**.

THE WEIGHING OF THE HEART CEREMONY
7 6 5 4 5 5 7 6 5 1 7 2 6 7 6 5 6 5 1 5 7 3 5 5 5 1 2 1 2 = **132**

The first thing we can find in the Weighing of the Heart Ceremony is our Holy 108 of Phi. In Volume 1, we covered this very sacred number in depth (see p. 15-18, shown again below) and saw its importance in many spiritualities ranging from Islam to Buddhism to Taoism. Since we know that *The Weighing of the Heart* is indeed a ceremony, we can drop the word *Ceremony*, summing to 24 and find our Holy **108**.

THE WEIGHING OF THE HEART
7 6 5 4 5 5 7 6 5 1 7 2 6 7 6 5 6 5 1 5 7 = **108**

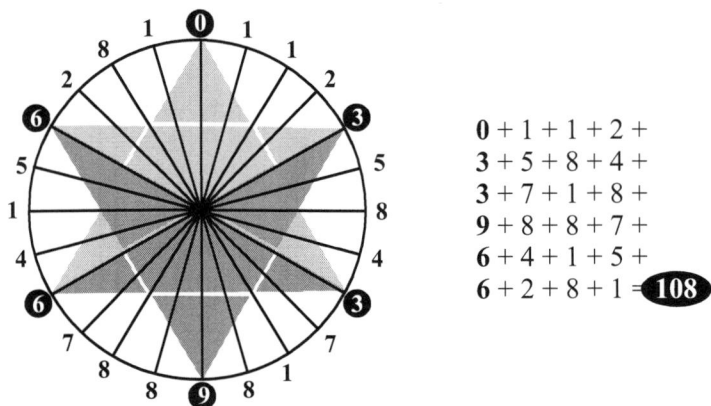

$$0 + 1 + 1 + 2 +$$
$$3 + 5 + 8 + 4 +$$
$$3 + 7 + 1 + 8 +$$
$$9 + 8 + 8 + 7 +$$
$$6 + 4 + 1 + 5 +$$
$$6 + 2 + 8 + 1 = \textbf{108}$$

Dropping the word *The* from *The Weighing of the Heart* gives us the **90** degrees of a right angle and leads us right back to our mirrored number line, or adding the numbers 0-9 (0 + 1 + 2 + 3 + 4 + 5 + 6 + 7 + 8 + 9 = 45) as well as to the Hermetic principle of correspondence, the very philosophy embedded in the Seal of Solomon.

WEIGHING OF THE HEART
4 5 5 7 6 5 1 7 2 6 7 6 5 6 5 1 5 7 = **90**

9 8 7 6 5 4 3 2 1 ⓪ 1 2 3 4 5 6 7 8 9

AS ABOVE, SO BELOW   AS BELOW, SO ABOVE
1 6 1 2 2 5 5   6 2 2 5 2 2 4   1 6 2 5 2 2 4   6 2 1 2 2 5 5

45 → ⑨⓪ ← 45

In looking back at the **132** of *The Weighing of the Heart Ceremony* we can find the alchemical marriage encoded within this number. The divisors of **132** are 1, 2, 3, 4, 6, 11, 12, 22, 33, 44, 66, and 132. Adding these 12 digits together yields us the number **336** (1 + 2 + 3 + 4 + 6 + 11+ 12 + 22 + 33 + 44 + 66 + 132 = **336**). The number **336** is once again recognized in Jesus and his Disciples and the alchemical marriage of the *King* and the *Queen*.

♚ KING   x   ♛ QUEEN = 336

The division of the soul within must be unified in order to allow the spirit to ascend and hence make one's heart lighter than a feather.

The number **132** is also extremely interesting, for it references our earthly sphere. Since we are dealing with Egyptian lore, the Thrice Great Hermes and his knowledge of the trinity will come in handy. The **132** of *The Weighing of the Heart Ceremony* multiplied by our Holy Trinity equals **396** (132 x 3 = 396). This multiplied by your ten fingers sums to **3,960** - the radius of the Earth in miles.

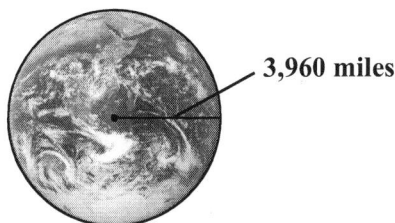

3,960 miles

Study of the natural world, especially through the seven liberal arts - grammar, rhetoric, logic, music, cosmology, number, and geometry - is quintessential in helping one understand oneself. Going into the *heart of nature* herself and getting a firm grip on her processes and workings will help one to understand the workings and magical nature of the self. Taking up study on these subjects is not enough though. If one undergoes the alchemical process without his heart leading him, it matters not how many books he reads or how much measuring he does, his pursuit will ultimately not yield him the fruits of spiritual nourishment. If power, greed, egotism, and self-rightouesness are the footsteps with which one walks the path, one will not find the entrance to the Lion's Gate. Only he with *the strong grip of a lion's paw* will find the gold within his temple.

Using our cipher we can weigh our *Heart* against a *Feather* and find not only *Jesus Christ*, a *Reborn Christian,* and the *Alchemical Marriage* but also *The Holy Name of God,* whose name in this instance, would be of course, *your name. Feather* sums to **35** and *Heart* sums to **24**, together equaling **59** (35 + 24 = **59**).

59

FEATHER   HEART
6 5 1 7 6 5 5 = **35**   6 5 1 5 7 = **24**

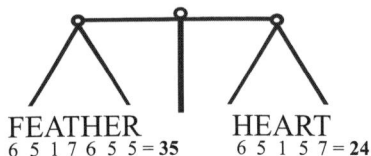

Jesus Christ, Reborn Christian, Alchemical Marriage, Alchemical Wedding, English Alphabet, Knights Templar, In God We Trust, The Holy Name of God

In Volume 1 we looked at the name of *Jesus Christ* in depth, understanding that the title Christ was a title available to all those who seek this enlightened state. Christhood is a state of grace, the completion of the alchemical process, the rebirth of the Christian, and the highest degree one may achieve in Freemasonry. All spiritualities speak of this ascension, and the core philosophy behind this sacred elevation lies within that wonderful Hermetic adage of "As Above, So Below." What is *above* in the Heavens, is *below*, or *within you*. The Kingdom of God resides *inside of you*. The microcosm reflects the macrocosm, they are a unified sphere. Intuiting this and taking this understanding into one's own heart is how one may achieve this awakening. The awakening, the Christhood, the enlightenment is understanding that you are indeed *equal to God, you are one and the same being*. We can find this absolute truth within the *Heart* and *Feather* as well. The difference between the **35** of Feather and the **24** of Heart is **11** (35 - 24 = **11**). The number eleven is nothing more than an equal sign standing upright, informing you of *your equality to God*. It is in fact telling you that EL is EVEN, or simply stated, *you are even with God* (El). These two ones also represent the gateway to the higher spiritual self, or the passageway to the glory of the kingdom of Heaven. It is no accident that *Heaven* and *eleven* rhyme and share the same numerical equivalent.

HEAVEN   ELEVEN
6 5 1 5 5 1 = **23** = 5 2 5 5 5 1

Go within to find the without and you will see that they are one and the same. Tread lightly, live passionately, find your bliss, and most importantly, *follow your heart,* for it will not steer you wrong.

So the question remains: *Does your heart weigh less than a feather?*

UNIDEUS

Modern science has been toying with the idea for sometime of a multiverse, that is that our universe is simply but one universe within a multitude of universes. Many postulate that within every black hole lies another universe and within that universe exists an infinite number of black holes. This mental game can continue on ad infinitum. Such thoughts can be quite overwhelming and can quickly give one a headache. Simple philosophy can help us solve this conundrum of the multitudes. In order to understand the infinite multitudinous nature of space and time, we have to look no further than the first whole number in existence, or *One*, to truly grasp what is going on.

Even if it were true that there is universe after universe existing within each black hole, it really matters not. We can exponentiate universe after universe, but ultimately we must eventually come to the conclusion that at some scale and at some level, they are unified. They are one *uni*verse. The human body consists of some 60 trillion sentient cells, each cell performing its particular function (and each a universe in and of itself), and yet all of these cells come together to form the *singular universe of you*. We can ruminate all day long on the number of verses we have, but we must recognize that invariably, these verses come together as one song. And that song is the harmony that we all participate in. We all help sing the song of the glory of our universe.

Each human life is a verse within the unified song of God.

There is but one god, one story, and one universe. Infinity is wrapped up within itself, and it matters not how far you send your thoughts, or how many digits of pi we calculate, or how far we travel into space, ultimately we will find ourselves back at the *One*. And this unifying *One* is the omnipotence, omniscience, and omnipresence of God. One does not need to understand the arduous equations of modern physics or travel light years into space to see, as plain as day, the simple fact that everything in the universe is connected. It is Whole. Holy. Unified. Divine and not divided. And we are given these short lives to not only glimpse its grandeur but also help sing its glorious song. There is no need to over-intellectualize these things. The further we stray from the *One*, the more complicated we will make it. The universe is complex indeed, but it is not complicated. In fact, one needs but *One* number to understand it.

When we count, we don't start at *zero*. We start at *one*. The zero is the circle, and the circle encapsulates the most amount of geometric space and the *one* contains the all of creation. The *zero* and *one* perform the same function. They both wish to tell you about the unified nature of existence.

Count yourself and make yourself count. No matter how many ones there are in existence, they are but One *and you are that One*. All aspects of creation come together to form the story and song of the universe. The universe is the expression of God's will because God indeed wished to express himself. God differentiated himself into matter, intentionally losing himself so that he could play the game of life and find himself *through you*. God **dis-memebered** himself so that we could link ourselves back, through the practice of religion (literally defined as *linking-back*) and go through the process of **remembering** *who we are*. And when one practices this natural religion, it requires no indoctrination, no dogma, no laws or rituals to perform it. At the end of this task, one will ultimately find himself *one with all of creation*. This is the beauty of our creation. It provides us with innumerable questions and countless paradoxes, but in the end, it has but *one* answer. And life is the time-frame in which it gives you to find that answer. And the answer to God's riddle is the most beautiful, profound, and glorious answer one could ever conceive. To find the answer to the *Mystery* of this existence, one must endure the *Quest* to find oneself. Luckily for you, the answer to that *mystery* is no further than looking down at your two hands. *You are, in fact, the answer.*

QUEST
4 6 5 6 7 = **28**

MYSTERY
1 2 6 7 5 5 2 = **28**

The Answer

Look around you and welcome yourself home. *This is your kingdome.*

"We are the ones we've been waiting for." - Hopi Prophecy

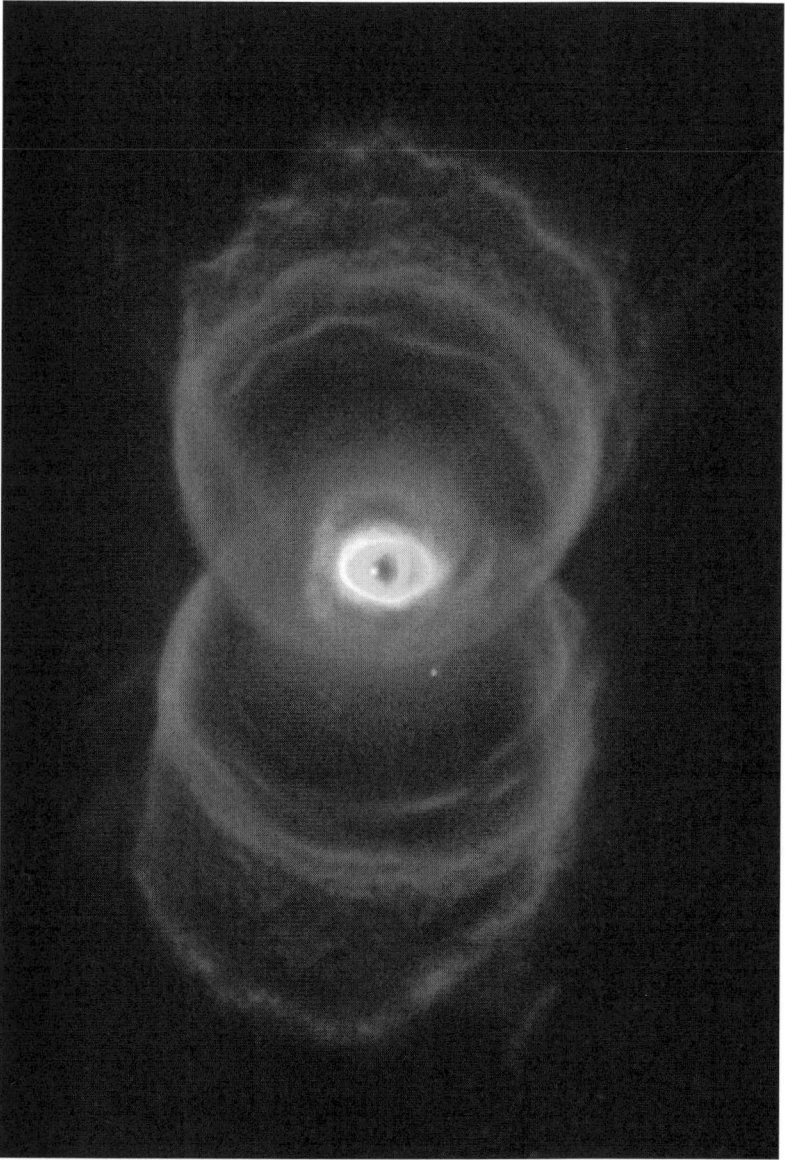

"What we are is God's gift to us. What we become is our gift to God."
~ Eleanor Powell

APPRECIATION

The Grand Architect

I

A Universal Picture

In order
to even to begin to understand
the nature of the idea
that we are divine,
inter-planetary,
multi-dimensional beings
spinning endlessly and endlessly
in the infinite
breath of time
that is now,
churning and churning
towards higher levels of awareness
one must make a valiant and quite heroic effort
to destroy all prior truths
and all normal senses,
all knowledge known
and all fed pretenses
and be willing without a single hesitation
to unlearn, de-program, dissolve,
everything he has come to trust and know,
take in as his own
and hold close as his comforts.
One must burn down his house,
fall asleep on the ashes,
and wake up appreciative of the chance he gets to
lie on the ground
and watch his life manifest in a dream.
For only then will he see
that the high water has already been rising,
that Rome's been falling nine times an hour
and that everything that's ever happened
is happening today.

~ Claudia Pavonis

HELPFUL RESOURCES

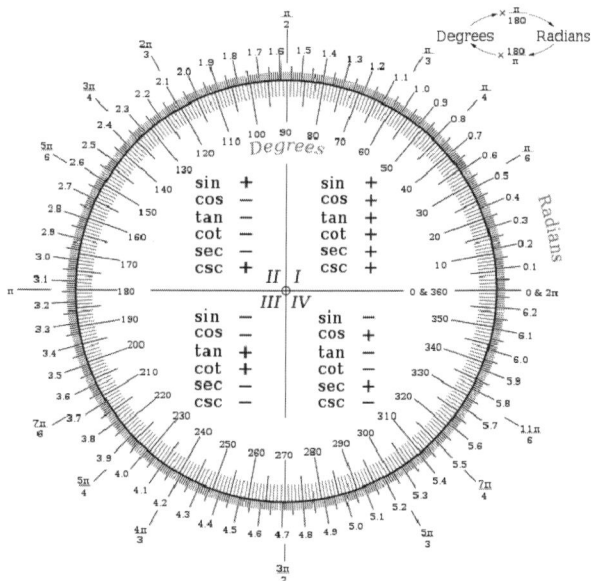

<table>
<tr><td></td><td>1</td><td>2</td><td>3</td><td>4</td><td>5</td><td>6</td><td>7</td><td>8</td><td>9</td></tr>
<tr><td>1</td><td>1</td><td>2</td><td>3</td><td>4</td><td>5</td><td>6</td><td>7</td><td>8</td><td>9</td></tr>
<tr><td>2</td><td>2</td><td>4</td><td>6</td><td>8</td><td>10</td><td>12</td><td>14</td><td>16</td><td>18</td></tr>
<tr><td>3</td><td>3</td><td>6</td><td>9</td><td>12</td><td>15</td><td>18</td><td>21</td><td>24</td><td>27</td></tr>
<tr><td>4</td><td>4</td><td>8</td><td>12</td><td>16</td><td>20</td><td>24</td><td>28</td><td>32</td><td>36</td></tr>
<tr><td>5</td><td>5</td><td>10</td><td>15</td><td>20</td><td>25</td><td>30</td><td>35</td><td>40</td><td>45</td></tr>
<tr><td>6</td><td>6</td><td>12</td><td>18</td><td>24</td><td>30</td><td>36</td><td>42</td><td>48</td><td>54</td></tr>
<tr><td>7</td><td>7</td><td>14</td><td>21</td><td>28</td><td>35</td><td>42</td><td>49</td><td>56</td><td>63</td></tr>
<tr><td>8</td><td>8</td><td>16</td><td>24</td><td>32</td><td>40</td><td>48</td><td>56</td><td>64</td><td>72</td></tr>
<tr><td>9</td><td>9</td><td>18</td><td>27</td><td>36</td><td>45</td><td>54</td><td>63</td><td>72</td><td>81</td></tr>
</table>

Standard Multiplication

<table>
<tr><td></td><td>1</td><td>2</td><td>3</td><td>4</td><td>5</td><td>6</td><td>7</td><td>8</td><td>9</td></tr>
<tr><td>1</td><td>1</td><td>2</td><td>3</td><td>4</td><td>5</td><td>6</td><td>7</td><td>8</td><td>9</td></tr>
<tr><td>2</td><td>2</td><td>4</td><td>6</td><td>8</td><td>1</td><td>3</td><td>5</td><td>7</td><td>9</td></tr>
<tr><td>3</td><td>3</td><td>6</td><td>9</td><td>3</td><td>6</td><td>9</td><td>3</td><td>6</td><td>9</td></tr>
<tr><td>4</td><td>4</td><td>8</td><td>3</td><td>7</td><td>2</td><td>6</td><td>1</td><td>5</td><td>9</td></tr>
<tr><td>5</td><td>5</td><td>1</td><td>6</td><td>2</td><td>7</td><td>3</td><td>8</td><td>4</td><td>9</td></tr>
<tr><td>6</td><td>6</td><td>3</td><td>9</td><td>6</td><td>3</td><td>9</td><td>6</td><td>3</td><td>9</td></tr>
<tr><td>7</td><td>7</td><td>5</td><td>3</td><td>1</td><td>8</td><td>6</td><td>4</td><td>2</td><td>9</td></tr>
<tr><td>8</td><td>8</td><td>7</td><td>6</td><td>5</td><td>4</td><td>3</td><td>2</td><td>1</td><td>9</td></tr>
<tr><td>9</td><td>9</td><td>9</td><td>9</td><td>9</td><td>9</td><td>9</td><td>9</td><td>9</td><td>9</td></tr>
</table>

Decimal Parity

THE EGYPTIAN ALPHABET

a	à	ā	i	u	b	p	f
m	n	r	h	ḥ	kh	kha	s
sh	q	k	g	t	th	ṭ	tch

REFERENCES & SOURCES

Opening page picture:
Musæum Hermeticum Reformatum et Amplificatum, 1625
Pictures, sources and illustrations, - www.wikipedia.com
All etymology - www.etymonline.com
All other illustrations / graphics created by Marty Leeds
Doubling the Cube explanation from Stephen Skinner's - Sacred Geometry:
Decipher the Code
Tau Cross explanation and Decimal Parity graphic (Helpful Resources)
from Scott Onstott - www.secretsinplainsight.com
Cat Eye Nebula, pg 129 from www.hubble.org

The following is a suggested reading list. An extra special thanks goes out to
all of these fantastic researchers. Many of the concepts, ideas and
philosophies within this volume were inspired by these works:

The Holy Bible - King James Version, Masonic Edition
A History of God - Karen Armstrong
Finnegans Wake - James Joyce
Te Tao Ching - Lao Tzu
Psychology and Alchemy - Carl Jung
Modern Man in Search of a Soul - Carl Jung
Man and His Symbols - Carl Jung
The Light of Egypt, Volume 1 & 2 - Thomas Burgoyne
The Alvin Boyd Kuhn Collection - Alvin Boyd Kuhn
The Esoteric Structure of the Alphabet and its Hidden Mystical
Language- Alvin Boyd Kuhn
Sacred Geometry - Stephen Skinner
Quadrivium (The Four Classic Liberal Arts of) - Keith Critchlow,
Miranda Lundy, David Sutton, Jason Martineau, John Martineau
Anthony Ashton
Taking Measure: Explorations in Number, Architecture and Consciousness -
Scott Onstott
Useful Mathematical & Physical Forumlae - Matthew Watkins
A Study of Numbers - R.A. Schwaller de Lubicz
The Theology of Arithmetic (Iamblichus) - Translated by Robin Waterfield
The Corpus Hermeticum - Translated by G.R.S. Mead
The Emerald Tablet of Hermes and The Kybalion - Edited by Dr. Jane Ma'ati
Smith C. Hyp. Msc. D.
The Secret Doctrine - Helena Blavatsky
Talisman - Graham Hancock and Robert Buvaul

The Secret Teaching of all Ages - Manly P. Hall
The Lost Keys of Freemasonry - Manly P. Hall
Sun, Moon and Earth - Robin Heath
The Science of the Dogon - Laird Scranton
The Cosmological Origin of Myth and Symbol - Laird Scranton
Myths to Live By - Joseph Cambell
The Hero With a Thousand Faces - Joseph Cambell
Lost Star of Myth and Time - Walter Cruttendon
Serpent In The Sky - John Anthony West
Aerodynamics Point Energy Creation Physics - Marko Rodin
Signs and Symbols - DK Publishing
The Lost Masonic Word - Dr. J.D. Buck
Through Indian Eyes, The Untold Story of Native American Peoples -
Editors of Reader's Digest
Lakota Star Theology, Studies in Lakota Stellar Theology - Ronald Goodman
Man's Search for Meaning - Viktor E. Frankl
Science and the Akashic Field - Ervin Laszlo
A Beginner's Guide to Constructing the Universe - Michael S. Schneider
How the World is Made - John Michell with Allan Brown
The Lost Science of Measuring the Earth - John Michell and Robin Heath
Knowledge of Higher Worlds and its Attainment - Rudolf Steiner
On Formally Undecidable Propositions of Principia Mathematica and
Related Systems - Kurt Goedel
Religion in the Making - Alfred North Whitehead
Pythagoras - Thomas Stanley
The Phenomenon of Man - Pierre Teilhard de Chardin
The Holy Science - Swami Sri Yukteswar
The Egyptian Book of the Dead - Chronicle Books
Alan Watts - This is It
Siddartha - Herman Hesse
God Has a Dream - Desmond Tutu
The Archaic Revival - Terence McKenna
The Gnostic Circle - Patrizia Norelli Bachelet
In a Sacred Manner I Live, Native American Wisdom - Edited by Neil Philip
A History of Western Philosophy - Betrand Russell
Wholeness and the Implicate Order - David Bohm
Cosmic Trigger - Robert Anton Wilson
The War of Art - Steven Pressfield
The Secret Language of Birthdays - Gary Goldschneider
God-Man: The Word Made Flesh - George W. Carey and Inez Eudora Perry
Zodiac and the Salts of Salvation - - George W. Carey and Inez Eudora Perry
Tree of Life, an Expose of Physical Regenesis - George W. Carey

Fingerprints of the Gods - Graham Hancock
Supernatural - Graham Hancock
Sacred Path Cards - Jamie Sans
Karl Anderson - The Astrology of the Old Testament

Lectures, Videos and Online Sources:

Hidden Meanings - Bill Donahue, www.hiddenmeanings.com
Secrets in Plain Sight - Scott Onstott, www.secretsinplainsight.com
Santos Bonacci - Lecture Series, www.universaltruthschool.com
Various lectures - "The Psychedelic Salon" with host Lorenzo
Johan Oldenkamp - Lecture Series, www.pateo.nl
Magical Egypt - John Anthony West
Quest for the Lost Civilization - Graham Hancock
Maybe Logic - Robert Anton Wilson
The Cross of Thoth - Crichton E. Miller
Joseph Cambell, Collected Lectures and The Power of Myth with Bill Moyers
www.jcf.org
Nassim Haramein - http//:theresonanceproject.org
Northern Exposure Television Series
www.wikipedia.com
http://alanwatts.com - Alan Watts, Life and Works
www.schooloftheholyscience.org
www.khanacademy.org
http://vihart.com - Vi Hart, Mathemusician

A special thank you to the editor William Summey.

Also available from Marty Leeds:
Pi - The Great Work
Pi & The English Alphabet Vol. 1
Music - Opus Medico Musica
Please visit: www.martyleeds33.com

THE END
7 6 5 5 1 4 = **28**

Printed in Great Britain
by Amazon.co.uk, Ltd.,
Marston Gate.